The Ramifications

of

Our Salvation

Eleutheros Books

*A series of Christian books
dedicated to two great causes:*

A revival of evangelism

and

A revival of Biblical thinking among God's people

Volume I:

The Ramifications

of

Our Salvation

*Including 4 quizzes, a final
exam, and an answer key*

The Ramifications

of

Our Salvation

By John Rataczak, Ph.D.

Eleutheros Books

*If the Son therefore shall make you free, ye shall
be free indeed* (John 8:36).

Printed in the United States

Books in the Eleutheros Series

Volume I: The Ramifications of Our Salvation

Future books:

Volume II: Bible Translations: A Closer Look

*Volume III: Spiritual Gifts Verse by Verse: A Commentary on
I Corinthians 12-14*

*Volume IV: 19th Century Influences on 21st Century
Christianity*

*Volume V: The Messages of Two Old Testament Prophets:
Amos and Micah*

*Volume VI: Biblical Foundations: A Commentary on
Genesis 1-11*

For future orders, go to www.eleutherosbooks.com

Contents

Dedication

To the memory of my father,

Edward Louis Rataczak:

loving parent,

educated engineer,

devoted husband,

friend to many,

sincere believer in Jesus Christ.

His words of wisdom and encouragement have been
a blessing to all who knew him.

The Ramifications of Our Salvation

Introduction

But as many as received Him, to them gave He power to become the sons of God, even to them that believe on His name (John 1:12).

Ask believers to speak about their salvation, and in most cases you'll find that they will do so gladly. Such discussions generally take on one of two themes:

#1. They will tell about the person who led them to Christ or mention the time and place where the miracle of the new birth occurred. Many times they will speak fondly of a pastor, missionary, friend, or Sunday School teacher who cared enough to take the time to present the good news of the Gospel to them. There also is often a high regard for the place where they experienced God's saving grace. It would be fair to say that to these people the *circumstances* of their salvation are very important.

#2. Others will readily recall how they reacted to the Gospel when they heard it or how they felt immediately after accepting Christ as Savior. Common sentiments are conviction of sin, love for Jesus, relief that their eternal destiny is now heaven instead of hell, or tears of joy. To these people the *emotions* involved in their salvation are very important.

Ask these same people to define the word "propitiation," and very few have any idea what it means. They might remember hearing this word in a sermon but cannot explain its significance. Ask these same people about justification, sealing, glorification, redemption, any number of other important Biblical words, and the reaction will be very similar. To state the case frankly, they have little *knowledge* about their salvation.

At this point we would do well to ask some simple questions. Should we rely primarily on circumstances and emotions to explain to others and ourselves what took place when we were saved? Are these things reliable? When we do that, are we not in some ways attempting to interpret Biblical truth by emotions/circumstances instead of interpreting emotions/circumstances by Biblical truth?

Having pondered these questions, we should draw three simple conclusions:

#1. The Bible is our only reliable source of information. It is inspired by the Holy Spirit, inerrant on all subjects, and authoritative. By "authoritative" we mean it is the only source we can use to determine what to do, what to be, and what to believe. Other sources have their limitations because they are based on mere human knowledge and/or opinions. Many Biblical references could be given here, but the following verses demonstrate the point:

We have a more sure word of prophecy; whereunto ye do well that ye take heed as unto a light that shineth in a dark place, until the day dawn, and the day star arise in your hearts. For the prophecy came not in old time by the will of man: but holy men of God spake as they were moved *by the Holy Ghost* (II Peter 1:19, 21).

For ever, O Lord, Thy Word is settled in heaven (Psalm 119:89).

#2. Emotions are very changeable. One well-known preacher, now with the Lord, used to say something like this: "I'm glad my salvation doesn't depend on my emotions because I don't *feel* saved until I've had a cup of coffee in the morning!" Apparently that coffee helped him "feel" saved, but nobody would argue that coffee adequately replaces the blood of Christ!

#3. How people interpret circumstances differs greatly. Take a look at news analysis and you'll find commentators agreeing on basic facts but reaching totally different conclusions regarding the significance of events or what the national/international reactions should be. People have varying opinions, but God's Word does not change!

The goal of this book is to explain in a clear way what happens Biblically the moment a believer is saved. The outline is simple:

I.   The Pre-Science of Our Salvation (God's Planning of it)
II.   The Privileges of Our Salvation
III. The Permanence of Our Salvation
IV.   The Practicality of Our Salvation

Please understand that God offers us a thorough salvation. The Scriptures declare that "we are complete in Him" (Colossians 2:10). The splendor of it is that all three Persons of the trinity are involved (more on this as the book progresses), and they have collectively worked from eternity past, through present times, and will continue their unified ministry forever in the final state.

To all three Persons be the glory forever!

This book is not intended to be a thorough systematic theology on all areas of soteriology (the doctrine of salvation), but rather an introduction to the important doctrines/concepts that believers everywhere should know and love.

Great care will be given to the Greek and Hebrew originals, but all Biblical quotes, unless otherwise noted, will be from the King James Version (KJV).

This author would like to offer a few words of personal note here. First, thank you for your interest in this book and its subject matter. Second, please be aware that a simple knowledge of Biblical doctrines is not always very helpful. In fact, such an approach can easily bring on an arrogance that is quite offensive. Biblical knowledge is important, but it must be accompanied by the desire to become more Christ-like in our attitudes and actions.

The Apostle Paul made this very clear when writing to the church at Corinth:

Whether therefore ye eat, or drink, or whatsoever ye do, do *all to the glory of God* (I Corinthians 10:31).

Any mistakes in spelling or grammar are the sole responsibility of this author.

Was it for crimes   **At the Cross**
That I have done,   Isaac Watts
He groaned upon the tree?
Amazing pity,
Grace unknown!
And love beyond degree!

Section I: The Pre-Science of Our Salvation

Overview

As Thou hast given Him power over all flesh, that He should give eternal life to as many as Thou hast given Him (John 17:12).

Although there is consistent agreement among Christians that God has devised a plan of salvation in general, there is considerable debate about its specific details.

On these points all agree: God the Father sent His Son Jesus Christ into the world. He was virgin born, lived a sinless life, bore the sins of the world in His body while dying on the cross, shed His blood to pay for mankind's salvation, and rose from the grave on the third day. Those who repent of their sins and place their faith solely in Him are immediately saved by the grace of God, and an eternity in heaven with Him and others who have likewise believed is assured.

That having been said, several questions arise. Did God plan ahead of time the salvation of every believer? If so, does that mean only certain ones will be saved? Can such a plan be considered fair? Can such a plan be demonstrated Biblically?

It is not the intent of this author to offend any who may come from backgrounds in which they were taught differently (and therefore may disagree with him on certain points), but rather to present the truth in love. There are many on both sides of this issue, and in reality the only way to resolve it is to look closely at what Scripture teaches.

To answer the question about fairness, first consider Noah and his situation. In Genesis 6:5-7 it is clear that man's sin in Noah's day was very wicked. It was so offensive to God that He said,

I will destroy man whom I have created from the face of the earth, both man and beast....

Some might say that it was *unfair* for God to say such about the entire human race. Should He not have given sinful man more of a chance to survive? To ask such a question, however well-intended it may be, is to misunderstand the nature of man's condition and the absolute holiness of God.

The Bible declares that

God is light, and in Him is no darkness at all (I John 1:5).

The point is that God cannot tolerate even one sin! His holiness simply will not allow such. It was only God's forbearance that allowed the people of Noah's day to live as long as they did. The same can and should be said about our world today!

And yet God, angry and disgusted at man's sin as He surely was, looked at one particular man (and his family) totally differently.

But Noah found *grace* in the eyes of the Lord (Genesis 6:8).

Was there something in Noah that made him better than everyone else on earth? Be careful in answering that question because the definition of grace is *unmerited* favor. The answer is that Noah was a sinner as all others. Read Genesis 9:19-29 to see the sin of Noah and his family even after the flood. To answer the question above, Noah was not better than all others of his day.

Some might ask if it was fair for God to choose Noah out of the millions, perhaps billions, of people who lived on the earth at that time. In fact, it might be appropriate to ask if it is "fair" for God to choose anybody for

All have sinned and come short of the glory of God (Romans 3:23).

Serious issues as these require a suitable solution. The Biblical answer is that *God is better than fair* because He shows grace! Thank God for that, because if God were "fair" with mankind, He would treat us all equally and give us exactly what we deserve. The Apostle Paul declares

For the wages of sin is death… (Romans 6:23a).

It is clear that some need to understand more completely what is involved in God's sovereignty (His absolute lordship over creation). Romans 9 is an important passage on this subject.

What shall we say then? Is there unrighteousness with God? God forbid. For He saith to Moses, I will have mercy on whom I will have mercy, and I will have compassion on whom I will have compassion. So that it is not of him that willeth, nor of him that runneth, but of *God that sheweth mercy* (Romans 9:14-16).

Therefore hath He mercy on whom He will have mercy, and whom He will he hardeneth. Thou wilt say then unto me, Why doth He yet find fault? For who hath resisted His will? Nay, but, O man, who art thou that repliest against God? Shall the thing formed say to him that formed it, Why hast thou made me thus? *Hath not the potter power over the clay*, over the same lump to make one vessel unto honor, and another vessel unto dishonor (Romans 9:18-21)?

The Apostle Paul asks a very significant question in verse 20: "who art thou that repliest against God?" What man is there who has such authority, intelligence, or holiness? To put it another way, what legal body in all the universe has the moral standing to tell the eternal God of all creation what is and what is not fair?!

6

Preposterous imagination!

We are forced by all this to say that God is not under any obligation to be "fair" and that nobody even has the right to question that fact.

Just as surely, we are compelled by Biblical truth to fall on hands and knees daily, and with hearts full of love and praise for our Savior, to proclaim, "My God, how great Thou art!"

The second question was whether or not it is Biblical to believe God chose ahead of time each individual who is saved. The answer to this legitimate question is a simple "yes," and the Biblical support for this affirmation is found in God's foreknowledge, election, and predestination. These subjects, making up the next three chapters, are the pre-science of our salvation.

Just a word of caution here. A little knowledge on a Biblical subject can be a dangerous thing. Perhaps this simple illustration will help.

Imagine there is a young couple in your church that is planning to be married soon. The young man decides to study the Bible to see what it says about marriage. His investigation brings him to Ephesians 5:22-24, but that is the extent of his awareness of Biblical teaching on marriage. Clearly, nobody can learn all the Scriptural teaching from just three verses.

Here is what he has read:

Wives, submit yourselves unto your own husbands, as unto the Lord. For the husband is the head of the wife, even as Christ is the head of the church: and He is the Savior of the body. Therefore as the church is subject unto Christ, so let the wives be to their own husbands in every thing.

Nobody would argue that the young man had learned Biblical truth, but since that is *all* he knows on marriage, it would be very likely that major problems/misconceptions develop because of insufficient knowledge. Obviously, partial knowledge about any subject in the Scriptures can create difficulties. The young man needs also to understand verses 25-31 of Ephesians 5. He is to love his wife as

Christ loved the church and gave Himself for it (verse 25).

That same young man would also do well to read I Corinthians 13 to understand how demanding God's love *(agape)* really is. Real love

Suffereth long, and is kind (13:4), is not easily provoked (13:5), and beareth all things, believeth all things, hopeth all things, endureth all things (13:7). Furthermore, it never fails (13:8)!

If that young man fully understands and obeys the complete teaching on love and marriage, the ideas of "making his wife submit or else" will not enter his mind.

The same things can be said about the pre-science of our salvation. Overemphasis on God's planning of it (without the knowledge and appreciation of all teaching on this subject) can lead one to think that since God planned it all before the world began that man is basically a "robot" on this earth and has no responsibilities once he is saved. After all, God did it all, and since we are merely the recipients of His grace, it appears that we can ignore living a holy life, serving God, or telling others about "so great salvation."

If all we knew or emphasize about salvation is God's planning of it, then misconceptions, unbiblical attitudes, arrogance, and other sins could easily enter into our lives just as the partial knowledge or emphasis on one point in marriage could easily create major problems for the young man and his soon-to-be wife in the illustration above.

The pre-science of our salvation is a precious subject, but it must be balanced with all the relevant Biblical teaching.

He loved me ere I knew Him,
And all my love is due Him!
He plunged me to victory
Beneath the cleansing flood!

Victory in Jesus
E.M. Bartlett

I

He Foreknew Us

For whom He did foreknow, He also did predestinate to be conformed to the image of His Son (Romans 8:29).

One inescapable fact is that God knows far more than man. To say it simply, God knows all things; man knows some things. Perhaps the following illustration will explain this.

Serious baseball fans know quite a bit about their favorite teams and players. They can explain to anyone who will listen such things as how many World Series titles their team has won, what the lifetime batting average of its best players were, and what the names of all the regular players were for the past several years.

Sometimes these fans seem to have a never ending knowledge, but even the most aware fans cannot give the same information about all the other teams in major league baseball.

When it comes to foreknowledge, all a fan can do is "guess" about things. For instance, will the 7:00 game tomorrow night start on time or will there be a rain delay? Which team will win and what will the final score be? How many hits will the first baseman get in that game?

Quite obviously, no mere fan can know all the history or foreknow all the future of baseball.

God, however, knows AND foreknows all things. Consider the following Biblical facts about these subjects.

God knows all things.
1. He knows man's thoughts.
   O Lord, Thou hast searched me, and known me. Thou *knowest* my downsitting and mine uprising, Thou *understandest* my thought afar off. Thou compassest my path... (Psalm 139:1-3a).

2. He knows man's needs.
   Be not ye therefore like unto them: for your Father *knoweth* what things ye have need of, before ye ask Him (Matthew 6:8).

3. He knows man's works.
   The Lord looketh from heaven; He beholdeth the sons of men. From the place of His habitation *He looketh upon the inhabitants of the earth.* He fashioneth their hearts alike; He considereth all their works (Psalm 33:13-15).

4. He knows all about His vast creation.
    He telleth the number of the stars; *He calleth them all by their names* (Psalm 147:4).

5. He knows all spiritual things.
    O the depth of the riches both of the wisdom and knowledge of God! *How unsearchable are His judgments* and His ways past finding out! For who hath known the mind of the Lord? Or who hath been His counsellor (Romans 11:33-34)?

6. He knows every detail about man.
    But *the very hairs of your head* are numbered (Matthew 10:30).

7. He knows about the *possibilities* of events.
    Woe unto thee, Chorazin! Woe unto thee, Bethsaida! For if the mighty works which were done in thee had been done in Tyre and Sidon, *they would have repented long ago* in sackcloth and ashes (Matthew 11:21).

    And thou, Capernaum, which art exalted in heaven, shalt be brought down to hell: For if mighty works which have been done in thee had been done in Sodom, *it would have remained until this day* (Matthew 11:23).

8. He knows all things!
    I know that Thou canst do every thing, and that *no thought can be withholden from Thee* (Job 42:2).

God foreknows all things.

1. He knew about the crucifixion of His Son before creation.
    Him, being delivered by *the determinate counsel and foreknowledge of God*, ye have taken, and by wicked hands have crucified and slain (Acts 2:23).

    Forasmuch as ye know that ye were not redeemed with corruptible things, as silver and gold, from your vain conversation received by tradition from your fathers; But with the precious blood of Christ, as of a lamb without blemish and without spot: Who verily was *foreordained before the foundation of the world*, but was manifest in these last times for you. (I Peter 1:18-19).

2. His foreknowledge is infinite.
    Great is our Lord, and of great power: *His understanding is infinite* (Psalm 147:5).

    Neither is there any creature that is not manifest in His sight: but all things are naked and opened unto the eyes of Him with Whom we have to do (Hebrews 4:13).

God foreknows who will be saved.

> Peter, an apostle of Jesus Christ, to the strangers scattered throughout Pontus, Galatia, Cappadocia, Asia, and Bythinia, Elect *according to the foreknowledge of God the Father...* (I Peter 1:1-2).

> *For whom He did foreknow,* He also did predestinate to be conformed to the image of His Son... (Romans 8:29a).

Immortal, invisible,
God only wise,
In light inaccessible
Hid from our eyes,
Most blessed, most glorious,
The Ancient of days,
Almighty, victorious,
Thy great name we praise!

Immortal, Invisible, God Only Wise
Walter Chalmers Smith

II

He Chose Us

Paul, an apostle of Jesus Christ by the will of God, to the saints which are at Ephesus, and to the faithful in Christ Jesus: According as He hath chosen us in Him before the foundation of the world... (Ephesians 1:1, 4).

Those of us who live in the western world are used to making choices. We choose our governmental officials every so often. We also make choices about many other things that affect our lives. Examples of this would be if and when to further our education, if and when to marry, what kind of job/career to pursue, even (within budgetary limits) where we would like to live.

God made man with a will and the capability to make choices. John 1:13 speaks of the "will of the flesh" and "the will of man."

Just as clearly as both the Bible and normal experience teach us that we humans can make choices, it is even more apparent that God makes choices as well.

It is obvious, for instance, that God *chose* to create all things:

All things were made by Him, and *without Him was not any thing made that was made* (John 1:3).

Nobody persuaded God to perform creation, and nobody helped Him do it. In fact, in Genesis 1:3

God said, Let there be light, and there was light.

This verse speaks of God's infinite wisdom and power, but also of one of the choices He made in creation.

God could have made the entire universe in some other way or at a different "time" which would have been known only to Him, but we have the revelation from Him in His Word that He employed six days to create the earth and all that is in it (Genesis 1-2).

God was under no obligation to create birds, but He chose to do so. For that matter, nobody was there to tell Him to create or not create man, but He chose to do that also.

John 3:16-17 reveals that God decided to send His sinless Son to die for sinful man:

For God so loved the world that *He gave His only begotten Son,* that whosoever believeth in Him should not perish, but have everlasting life. For God sent not His Son into the world to condemn the world: but that the world through Him might be saved.

The word "so" in this verse means *in this way*, not *so much*. There is no doubt that God loved mankind very deeply and dearly, but the idea of *so* here actually strongly suggests a plan of salvation that He made long before man was ever created.

Thus far we have seen that God makes choices and that these choices include such things as creation and the plan to send His Son Jesus to die for the sins of the world. The question then arises: did God choose those who would be saved? Although there is some controversy about this subject, the Scriptures give an unambiguous answer.

Before giving the Biblical evidence about God's answer, we would do well to acknowledge three basic tenets to which all Christians agree:

1. ***God must take the initiative in salvation.***
   We love Him *because He first loved us* (I John 4:19).

   For by grace are ye saved through faith; and that not of yourselves: *it is the gift of God;* Not of works, lest any man should boast (Ephesians 2:8-9).

2. ***Man, even in his helpless state, is responsible.***
   The following verses urge sinful man to turn to a holy God.

   Turn ye unto Him from Whom the children of Israel have deeply revolted (Isaiah 31:6).

   Therefore say unto the house of Israel, Thus saith the Lord God; *Repent, and turn yourselves from your idols; and turn away your faces* from all your abominations (Ezekiel 14:6).

   Because that which may be known of God is manifest in them; for God hath shown it unto them. For the invisible things of Him from the creation of the world are clearly seen, being understood by the things that are made, even His eternal power and Godhead; so that *they are without excuse* (Romans 1:20).

3. ***God's choices are not based on caprice or arbitrary will, but on His love and holiness.***

   God is *love* (I John 4:8b).

   Be ye therefore holy, *for I am holy* (Leviticus 11:45).

   These two verses indicate much about God's character. He simply cannot do anything or make any decision without balancing His love and holiness perfectly. He is also *immutable*. That means He will not and cannot ever change anything in His nature! These facts make it clear that God's choices are always consistent with Who He is.

Now consider whether or not God chose those who would be saved. Our Lord told His disciples,

Ye have not chosen Me, *but I have chosen you,* and ordained you… (John 15:16).

God told Ananias that the murderer Saul (later called Paul) was

A chosen vessel unto Me, to bear My name before the Gentiles, and kings, and the children of Israel (Acts 9:15).

Finally, the Apostle Peter, inspired by the Holy Spirit, describes believers as

A chosen generation, a royal priesthood, an holy nation, a peculiar people (I Peter 2:9a).

Other verses make the same point. In His holy and loving will He has decided to save whom He will.

Therefore hath He mercy *on whom He will have mercy,* and whom He will He hardeneth (Romans 9:18).

Unto you therefore which believe He is precious: but unto them which be disobedient, the stone which the builders disallowed, the same is made the head of the corner, And a stone of stumbling, and a rock of offense, even to them which stumble at the Word, being disobedient: whereunto also *they were appointed* (I Peter 2:8).

Some might ask, Why does God choose in this matter? Two simple answers may be given:

#1. If man somehow chose God rather than God's actually choosing man, then man would legitimately receive some of the glory for his own salvation.

#2. God has a will and exercised it, just as we humans do.

Why would He choose us? The only possible answers are His great love and truly amazing grace!

Jesus, lover of my soul,
Let me to Thy bosom fly,
While the nearer waters roll,
While the tempest still is high!
Hide me, O my Savior, hide
Till the storm of life is past;
Safe into the haven's guide,
O receive my soul at last!

Plenteous grace with Thee is found,
Grace to cover all my sin;
Let the healing streams abound,
Make and keep me pure within.
Thou of life the fountain art—
Freely let me take of Thee;
Spring Thou up within my heart,
Rise to all eternity!

Jesus, Lover
of My Soul
Charles Wesley

III

He Predestinated Us

But we speak the wisdom of God in a mystery, even the hidden wisdom which
God ordained before the world unto our glory
(I Corinthians 2:7).

From time to time we humans attempt to "predestinate" certain things. For instance, if you have a job that starts at 8:00 AM, you plan to go to bed at a certain time, to set an alarm clock to go off at a certain time, to be dressed suitably for the job by a certain time, and to arrive at the place of employment at the appropriate time.

Of course, there are times when even our best plans do not work very well. Who knew the electricity would go off, causing you to wake up at a different time than originally planned? Perhaps you receive an emergency phone call just as you were about to go out the door. Traffic jams, weather conditions, and many other unforeseen circumstances enter into the picture at times; and the plan, however well-intended, has to be modified accordingly.

When God predestinates something, however, we can be sure that it will happen every time *just as He planned.* The reasons for this are His foreknowledge and sovereignty.

The word "predestinate" comes from two Greek words. The preposition *pro* (which means "beforehand") and the verb *horkizo* (which means "to mark off by boundaries, to appoint") are combined in the word here.

The main verb *horkizo* is used to describe the designation of borders and the cities for the Levites in early Hebrew history (Numbers 34:6); God's appointment of the bounds of habitation for mankind (Acts 17:26); and a determination by the disciples to send financial aid to the brethren in Judea (Acts 11:29).

The compound word (to predestinate) is used primarily to speak of God's planning of man's salvation. The Apostle Paul uses this verb occasionally in His epistles to the churches of the first century:

For we are His workmanship, created in Christ Jesus unto good works, *which God hath before ordained* that we should walk in them (Ephesians 2:10).

For whom He did foreknow, *He also did predestinate* to be conformed to the image of His Son, that He might be the firstborn among many brethren. Moreover, whom He did predestinate, them He also called; and whom He called, them He also justified: and whom He justified, them He also glorified (Romans 8:29-30).

Three additional points should be made here:

1. ***God surely is never surprised when a sinner is saved.***
    He foreknew it, He chose for it to happen, and He foreordained it.

2. ***God's predestination of our salvation is conditional.***
    Although there is considerable debate in certain theological circles as to whether or not election and predestination are unconditional, the meanings of the verb "foreknow" and the noun "foreknowledge" are clear. They simply mean "to have knowledge in advance" and nothing more. A careful study of all the uses of "foreknow" in Greek literature reveals it *always* means "to foreknow," not to predestinate.

    Although God could have elected and predestinated without any conditions, the Scriptures indicate that He did not do so. Some would argue that "foreknow" means "to predestinate" in Romans 8:29 and I Peter 1:2, but the actual meaning of the word will not legitimately allow such an interpretation.

3. ***In God's mind, a believer's salvation was accomplished before creation.***
    Reread Romans 8:29-31.

I sing the mighty power of God
That made the mountains rise,
That spread the flowing seas abroad
And built the lofty skies.
I sing the wisdom that ordained
The sun to rule the day;
The moon shines full at His command,
And all the stars obey!

I Sing the Mighty
Power of God
Isaac Watts

Section II: The Privileges of Our Salvation
Overview

But as it is written, Eye hath not seen, nor ear heard, neither have entered into the heart of man, the things which God has prepared for them that love Him (I Corinthians 2:9).

Having determined that God planned man's salvation very thoroughly before He created all things, we now consider the things that happen to a believer from the moment he accepts Christ as Savior.

The list of doctrines connected to salvation is quite impressive, but before we begin the journey into these glorious truths, we would do well to ponder a few Biblical ideas. Below is a list that should prove helpful.

1. ***Our salvation was not cheap!***
   Forasmuch as ye know that ye were not redeemed with corruptible things, as silver and gold, from your vain conversation, received by tradition from your fathers; but with *the precious blood of Christ, as of a lamb without blemish* (I Peter 1:18-19a).

2. ***When God creates something, it is always good!***
   And God saw everything that He had made, and behold, *it was very good* (Genesis 1:31a).

   Of course sin causes disastrous problems, but a regenerated soul (a new creation in Christ) needs not fear eternal damnation:

   There is therefore now *no condemnation to them which are in Christ Jesus,* who walk not after the flesh, but after the Spirit (Romans 8:1).

3. ***Jesus came to save!***
   For the Son of man is come *to seek and to save* that which was lost (Luke 19:10).

4. ***Our salvation is paid in full!***
   When Jesus therefore had received the vinegar, He said, *It is finished:* and He bowed His head, and gave up the Ghost (John 19:30).

5. ***Jesus is the only way to be saved!***
   Jesus saith unto him, I am the way, the truth, and the life; *no man cometh unto the Father, but by Me. If ye had known Me, ye should have known My Father also* (John 14:6-7a).

6. ***Nothing is to be added to our salvation!***
   Consider the following illustration. One morning you decide to purchase a new car. You go to a number of dealerships, compare prices, consider the various models, sizes, and features of the various brands, test drive the two or three

18

that interest you the most, and finally fill out seemingly endless paperwork once you have made your selection.

No doubt there were a number of factors that entered into your final decision. Price is certainly an issue. You probably have strong preferences for certain features: these could include anything from GPS systems to anti-lock brakes.

Finally, you drive the car off the lot. What happens next?
1. The car depreciates in value.
2. The car will soon require maintenance.
3. The car needs gas in its tank.
4. The car must be insured.
5. The car will be recalled unless you meet payments.

Your "perfect" car becomes rather "imperfect" before too long, but we surely cannot say our salvation is lacking in any way! Take a close look at the five listings above and compare them to what God offers in salvation. There really is no comparison!

Regarding #1, can anybody honestly say that their salvation depreciates in value?

Blessed be the God and Father of our Lord Jesus Christ, which according to His abundant mercy hath begotten us again unto a lively hope by the resurrection of Jesus Christ from the dead, To an inheritance *incorruptible, and undefiled, and that fadeth not away, reserved in heaven for you* (I Peter 1:4).

Concerning #2, Christians are to "work out your own salvation with fear and trembling" (Philippians 2:12), but they are also told that God works in the lives of His own in such a way as to maintain their salvation:

For it is *God which worketh in you* both to will and do of His good pleasure (Philippians 2:13).

Being confident of this very thing, that He which hath begun a good work in you *will perform it until the day of Jesus Christ:* Even as it is meet for me to think this of you all... (Philippians 1:6-7a).

In other words, while man does have responsibilities, it is God Who takes care of the maintenance of our salvation.

As for #3, our Lord said to the woman at the well,

But whosoever drinketh of the water that I shall give him *shall never thirst; but the water I shall give him shall be a well of water springing up into everlasting life* (John 4:14).

God supplies the sustenance of our salvation. Obviously we humans need to put gas in the tank of our cars from time to time.

Considering #4, what we saw in the preceding chapters indicates clearly that a holy, omniscient, loving God made our salvation sure.

Looking at #5, when Jesus shed His blood on the cross, no more payments were necessary!

So Christ was *once offered* to bear the sins of many (Hebrews 9:28a).

The simple truth is this: God's provision in salvation is far greater than anything we can imagine!

And when, before the throne
I stand in Him complete,
Jesus died my soul to save,
My lips shall still repeat.

Jesus paid it all,
All to Him I owe;
Sin had left a crimson stain,
He washed it white as snow!

Jesus Paid it All
Elvina M. Hall

IV

Regeneration

Therefore if any man be in Christ, he is a new creature: old things are passed away; behold, all things are become new (II Corinthians 5:17).

In John 3:1-21 Jesus and Nicodemus have one of the most interesting conversations in all the Word of God. Early in the discussion,

Jesus answered and said unto him, Verily, verily I say unto thee, Except a man be *born again,* he cannot see the kingdom of God (John 3:3).

The word translated "again" in John 3:3 actually means "from above." As the discussion continues, it becomes obvious that Nicodemus understands that Jesus is talking about a miracle of some kind, but he does not correctly fathom the ideas of salvation and a new birth.

Actually, neither unsaved man nor angels totally understand all that is involved in regeneration.

The natural man receiveth not the things of the Spirit of God: for they are foolishness unto him; *neither can he know them,* because they are spiritually discerned (I Corinthians 2:14-15).

Regarding angels, the Scriptures indicate that they also lack understanding about the miracle of salvation. After all, Christ died for mankind, not the angels! Consider what the Apostle Peter was inspired to write on this subject:

Receiving the end of your faith, even the salvation of your souls. Of which salvation the prophets have inquired and searched diligently, who prophesied of the grace that should come unto you: Searching what, or what manner of time the Spirit of Christ which was in them did signify, when it testified beforehand the sufferings of Christ, and the glory that should follow. Unto whom it was revealed, that not unto themselves, but unto us they did minister the things, which are now reported unto you by them that have preached the Gospel unto you with the Holy Ghost sent down from heaven: *which things the angels desire to look into* (I Peter 1:9-12).

With the Holy Spirit's help and a systematic study of the Word we can see that the following points are true:

1. **Man is in desperate need of salvation.**
This is demonstrated by what our Lord said to Nicodemus in John 3:7,

Marvel not that I said unto thee, *Ye must be born again.*

The word *must* literally means "it is binding." Thus it is clear that Jesus insists on the necessity of the new birth. This is an indication of the sovereignty of our Lord.

Why is man in such need? The Scriptures teach that our natural condition is offensive to a holy God.

First, we are sinners who have disobeyed Him.
For *all have sinned, and come short of the glory of God* (Romans 3:23).

Second, we are without strength to change our situation.
For when we were yet *without strength,* in due time Christ died for the ungodly (Romans 5:16).

Third, God considers unsaved man
Dead in trespasses and sins (Ephesians 2:1b).

Obviously, in order to live, a dead person must be made alive again! This is what regeneration involves. Unfortunately, there are some who seem to feel that all unsaved man needs is a "dose of the right medicine," and all will be well. The new birth is a miracle that comes only from God, and to Him be all the glory!

Fourth, God considers man to be following Satan.
The field is the world; the good seed are the children of the kingdom; but the tares are *the children of the wicked one* (Matthew 13:38).

In this the children of God are manifest, and *the children of the devil:* whosoever doeth not righteousness is not of God, neither he that loveth not his brother (I John 3:10).

And said, O full of all subtlety and all mischief, *thou child of the devil,* thou enemy of all righteousness, wilt thou not cease to pervert the right ways of the Lord (Acts13:10)?

2. ***The Holy Spirit is the effective Agent in regeneration.***
Not by works of righteousness which we have done, but according to His mercy He saved us, by the *washing of regeneration and renewing of the Holy Ghost* (Titus 3:5).

3. ***The Word of God is also powerful in accomplishing regeneration.***
Of His own will *begat He us with the Word of truth* (James 1:18a).

Being born again, not of corruptible seed, but of incorruptible, *by the Word of God,* which liveth and abideth for ever. For all flesh is as grass, and the glory of man as the flower of grass (I Peter 1:23-24a).

4. **Regeneration is an act of the will of God.**
   Which were born, not of blood, nor of the will of the flesh, nor of the will of man, *but of God* (John 1:13).

5. **Regeneration causes radical changes in the lives of believers.**
   Four will be listed here.
   First, a believer receives power to overcome temptation.
   Whosoever is born of God *doth not commit sin:* for his seed remaineth in him: and he cannot sin, because he is born of God (I John 3:9).

   The words for "sin" in this verse are in the present tense in the Greek which means that the action would be continual. The implication is that a believer is, with God's help, able to overcome temptation in this life.

   Second, a believer loves his fellow believers.
   Whosoever believeth that Jesus is the Christ is born of God: and every one that loveth Him that begat *loveth him also that is begotten of Him* (I John 5:1).

   Third, a believer is obedient to God.
   By this we know that we are the children of God, when we love God, and *keep His commandments* (I John 5:2).

   Fourth, a believer loves God's Word.
   As newborn babes, *desire the sincere milk of the Word,* that ye may grow thereby (I Peter 2:2).

As Paul indicates in II Corinthians 5:17, a believer is "a new creature." If somehow a dog were to become a cat, it would not act the same way, eat the same kinds of food, or make the same kind of sounds. It would in fact be a "new creature!" When a sinner is born again he will be a totally different person in the way he thinks, what his goals are, and what he values. There is no doubt that a believer is totally changed when he accepts Christ as Savior!

From the human side, the meaning of the new birth is generally referred to as "conversion;" from the Divine side it is called "regeneration." Regeneration may be properly defined as "the communication of Divine life to the soul" (I John 3:5) or the "implantation of a new nature" (II Peter 1:4).

In conclusion, this new spiritual life affects the believer's intellect, will, and emotions.

And have put on the new man, which is renewed *in knowledge* after the image of Him that created Him (Colossians 3:10).

Now the God of peace that brought again from the dead our Lord Jesus, that great Shepherd of the sheep, through the blood of the everlasting covenant, Make you perfect in every good work *to do His will,* working in you that which is well pleasing in His sight, through Jesus Christ; to Whom be glory for ever and ever. Amen (Hebrews 13:21).

Whom having not seen, ye love; in Whom, though now ye see Him not, yet believing, ye rejoice *with joy unspeakable and full of glory* (I Peter 1:8).

Ye Must Be Born Again
William T. Sleeper

A ruler once came to Jesus by night
To ask Him the way of salvation and light:
The Master made answer in words true and plain,
"Ye must be born again."

Ye must be born again,
Ye must be born again.
I verily, verily say unto thee,
Ye must be born again.

V

Redemption

Forasmuch as ye know that ye were not redeemed with corruptible things, as silver and gold, from your vain conversation received by tradition from your fathers: But with the precious blood of Christ, as of a lamb without blemish and without spot (I Peter 1:18-19).

In the Graeco-Roman world of the first century AD virtually every city of any size had what was commonly called an *agora*. The agora was "a place of assembly, a market place." The common activity in a city's agora was the purchasing of property or goods.

The Biblical picture is quite vivid. In our natural state
We are all as an unclean thing, and all our righteousnesses are as filthy rags (Isaiah 64:6).

In addition to our unclean condition, we are in the slave market of sin, and even though filthy in our condition, Christ redeemed us!

As glorious as this is, God's idea of redemption involves much more than just buying us. The Greek verb *lutroo* carries with it the idea of "release on receipt of a ransom." Thus redemption means we have been bought out of our sinful condition!

Who gave Himself for us, that He might redeem us from all iniquity, and purify unto Himself a peculiar people, *zealous of good works* (Titus 2:14).

Wherefore say unto the children of Israel, I am the Lord, and I will bring you out from under the burden of the Egyptians, and *I will rid you of their bondage* (Exodus 6:6a).

The following references summarize the New Testament uses of *agorazo* and *exagorazo*, giving us much information about the doctrine of redemption.

1. **Believers are redeemed from the curse of the Law.**
   Christ *hath redeemed us from the curse of the Law,* being made a curse for us: for it is written, Cursed is every one that hangeth on a tree (Galatians 3:13).

   But when the fulness of the time was come, God sent forth His Son, made of a woman, made under the Law, *To redeem them that were under the Law,* that we might receive the adoption of sons. And because ye are sons, God hath sent forth the Spirit of His Son into your hearts… (Galatians 4:4-6a).

2. **Believers are bought with a price.**
   For ye are *bought with a price:* therefore glorify God in your body, and in your spirit, which are God's (I Corinthians 6:20).

3. *Unfortunately, many will deny or ignore the redemption God offers.*
    But there were false prophets also among the people, even as there shall be false teachers among you, who privily shall bring in damnable heresies, *even denying the Lord that bought them,* and bring upon themselves swift destruction (I Peter 2:1).

4. *In the end, people will be redeemed from every nation on earth.*
    And they sung a new song, saying, Thou art worthy to take the book, and to open the seals thereof: for Thou wast slain, and hast redeemed us to God by Thy blood out of *every kindred, and tongue, and people, and nation* (Revelation 5:9).

5. *Redemption has great cleansing power.*
    After this I beheld, and lo, a great multitude, which no man could number, of all nations, and kindreds, and people, and tongues, stood before the throne, and before the Lamb, clothed with white robes, and palms in their hands; And one of the elders answered, saying unto me, What are these which are arrayed in white robes? And whence came they? And I said unto him, Sir, thou knowest, And he said unto me, These are they which came out of great tribulation, and *have washed their robes, and made them white in the blood of the Lamb* (Revelation 7:9, 13-14).

6. *The price of our redemption was Christ's precious blood.*
    Forasmuch as ye know that ye were not redeemed with corruptible things, as silver and gold, from your vain conversation received by tradition from your fathers: But with *the precious blood of Christ,* as of a lamb without blemish and without spot (I Peter 1:18-19).

7. *God insisted that the shedding of blood be the price of redemption.*
    ...and *without shedding of blood is no remission* (Hebrews 9:22).

To conclude, there are many people in the world today who would suggest that there are many ways to pay for our sin. They would have us believe that a church, baptism, a religious rite, or perhaps some special state into which a person enters by his own works will be sufficient to redeem us from sin and bring us to God.

Biblically, of course, this kind of thinking is false and must be vigorously attacked. Questions then come up. Why does it have to be the blood of Christ that redeems us? Why couldn't something else do the same thing? Is it possible that God would allow some other way?

The simplest way to answer this important question is to consider the nature of the Father and the Person of Jesus Christ.

God the Father is absolutely holy.
...and ye shall be holy; *for I am holy...* (Leviticus 11:44a).

Since God is holy, He cannot tolerate even one sin in our lives, and He surely cannot accept a sacrifice that is anything less than perfect.

On the other hand, the sacrifice that would pay for man's sin had to be the death of a man, not an animal:

For it is *not possible that the blood of bulls and of goats should take away sins* (Hebrews 10:4).

For if the *blood of bulls and goats,* and the ashes of an heifer sprinkling the unclean, sanctifieth to the purifying of the flesh: How much more shall the blood of Christ, Who through the eternal Spirit offered Himself without spot to God, purge your conscience from dead works to serve the living God (Hebrews 9:13-14)?

Thus the only satisfactory Redeemer had to be a perfect man, and that is the God-man, Jesus Christ! No church, religious leader, or even sincere individual, could possibly live up to such a high standard. And since God insists on the shedding of blood as well as a sinless human sacrifice, Jesus Christ's shed blood is the only way!

This is why, of course, we glory in the cross and our Savior's redemptive work.

I have a song I love to sing
Since I have been redeemed,
Of my Redeemer, Savior, King,
Since I have been redeemed.

Since I have been redeemed,
I will glory in His name!
Since I have been redeemed,
I will glory in my Savior's name!

Since I Have Been Redeemed
Edward O. Excell

VI

Sanctification

Sanctify them through Thy truth: Thy Word is truth (John 17:17).

Regeneration is the miracle of the new birth. It takes place at the moment of salvation and is accomplished by the Holy Spirit.

Redemption is the miracle that buys the believer out of the slave market of sin and places him into the possession of Christ. The blood of Christ paid for this marvelous transaction, and redemption becomes a finished reality the moment we are saved by God's grace.

Now we come to the doctrine of sanctification. This is a complex subject about which there are varying opinions, but the following points are undeniably Biblical:

1. ***There are several elements to the meaning of the word "sanctification."***
   The Hebrew verb *qadash* carries with it the ideas of "being separate from the world, consecrated to God, belonging to God." It is used to refer to persons, places, days, and objects of worship. The following verses will illustrate:

   Sanctify unto Me all the firstborn, whatsoever openeth the womb among the children of Israel, both of man and of beast: it is Mine (Exodus 13:2).

   And thou shalt *sanctify the beast of the wave offering,* and the shoulder of the heave offering, which is waived (Exodus 29:27a).

   And if aught of the flesh of the consecrations, or of the bread, remain unto the morning, then thou shalt burn the remainder with fire: it shall not be eaten, because it is holy. And thus shalt thou do unto Aaron, and to his sons, according to all things which I have commanded thee: *seven days shalt thou consecrate them* (Exodus 29:34-35).

   And I commanded the Levites that they should *cleanse themselves,* and that they should come and keep the gates, to sanctify the Sabbath day. Remember me, O my God, concerning this also, and spare me according to the greatness of Thy mercy (Nehemiah 13:22).

   The New Testament verb *hagiazo* means "to hallow" and is sometimes used in reference to the name of God:

   And He said unto them, Our Father which art in heaven, *Hallowed be Thy name.* Thy kingdom come. Thy will be done, as in heaven, so in earth, Give us this day our daily bread. And forgive us our sins... (Luke 11:2-4a).

The same verb is also used to describe the place God is to have in the hearts of His own:

But *sanctify the Lord God in your hearts:* and be ready always to give an answer to every man that asketh you a reason of the hope that is in you with meekness and fear (I Peter 3:15).

Hagiazo also means "to purify, to make holy." The following use of this verb refers to the church:

That he might *sanctify and cleanse it* with the washing of water by the Word (Ephesians 5:26).

In another passage Paul uses *hagiazo* to refer to a future sanctification of all believers:

And the very God of peace *sanctify you wholly;* and I pray God your whole spirit and soul and body be preserved blameless unto the coming of our Lord Jesus Christ (I Thessalonians 5:23).

The word "saint" that occurs from time to time in the New Testament is related and literally means "holy ones." Biblically speaking, a "saint" is not a person who has been deceased for hundreds of years, has performed demonstrated miracles, has been deemed worthy of a special standing, and has had an ecclesiastical body confer upon him a very special honor. A "saint," according to the Word of God, is simply one who is saved by the grace of God.

Now concerning the collection *for the saints,* as I have given order to the churches of Galatia… (I Corinthians 16:1).

2. Sanctification is closely connected to the will of God.

For this is the will of God, even your *sanctification*, that ye should abstain from fornication: That every one of you should know how to possess his vessel in sanctification and honor (I Thessalonians 4:3-4).

Much could be said about God's will in the lives of believers, but this and many other verses/passages make it obvious that God intends for saints to live holy lives and honor Him.

3. There is a sense in which believers are already sanctified.
By this we mean that those who are saved are *made holy* because of the miracle of positional sanctification.

Probably the clearest verse on this important subject is found in I Corinthians 1:

Paul, called to be an apostle of Jesus Christ through the will of God, and Sosthenes our brother, Unto the church of God which is at Corinth, *to them that are sanctified* in Christ Jesus, called to be saints, with all that in every place call upon the name of Jesus Christ our Lord, both theirs and ours (I Corinthians 1:1-2).

These verses make three important points:

First, "to them that are sanctified" is a perfect tense in the Greek. This tense indicates action which is already accomplished but also indicates results that continue to abide. This universally completed action is something that happened the very moment the people in the church at Corinth were saved. The continuing *result* of being made holy is a perfect standing before our holy God!

Second, notice the phrase "called to be saints" here. Those who have been sanctified (which happened at the moment of salvation) are also called "saints" in this verse.

Third, this holy standing is accomplished "in Christ." We cannot save ourselves, and we surely cannot make ourselves holy, but in salvation the holiness of Christ is imparted. When God the Father looks at a believer He does not see his sin but rather the sinless blood and sinless life of Christ applied!

4. ***There is a sense in which believers are being sanctified.***
The preceding discussion was about a past, completed action that gives the believer a holy *position* before God the Father. This aspect of sanctification is a process that continues throughout the earthly lives of believers and is often called *progressive* sanctification.

There are a number of verses which indicate the importance of progressive sanctification.
But *grow in grace,* and in the knowledge of our Lord and Savior Jesus Christ (II Peter 3:18a). Obviously, growth is an ongoing process, and so is this aspect of sanctification.

This process is to involve an increase in our love for one another (I Thessalonians 3:12), a cleansing of self in the fear of God (II Corinthians 7:1), and a transformation into the image of Christ (II Corinthians 3:18; Ephesians 4:11-16).

A word must be said here about the idea of "sinless perfection." While our position in Christ is holy, and we as believers are to grow spiritually, absolute perfection in our conduct during this life is unattainable.

If we say that we have no sin, *we deceive ourselves,* and the truth is not in us (I John 1:8).

The key to understanding this verse is the present tense in the verb "have." This tense clearly indicates continued action. As believers in Christ we always have a holy standing before God, and we are growing in our spiritual lives, but this verse leaves no doubt that our sin nature cannot be eradicated. If we try to convince ourselves or others that we are beyond the possibility of sinning in this life, "we deceive ourselves" according to this verse.

The glory belongs to God in sanctification, whether it is positional or progressive. It would be very easy for a person to become prideful (and therefore involved in sin) if he could make a claim to be sinlessly perfect even before getting to heaven.

Paul speaks of a tremendous ongoing spiritual battle in his life, even though he had been used so mightily by God.

For that which I do I allow not; for what I would, *that do I not;* but what I hate, *that do I.* If then I do that which I would not, I consent unto the law that it is good. Now then it is no more I that do it, but sin that dwelleth in me. For I know that in me (that is, in my flesh) dwelleth no good thing; for to will is present with me: but how to perform that which is good I find not. For the good that I would do I do not: but the evil that I would not, that I do. O wretched man that I am! Who shall deliver me from the body of this death (Romans 7:15-19, 24)?

God does offer forgiveness for the sin of believers, thus restoring the *fellowship* that He surely desires. This is conditioned on our confession of wrongdoing.

If we confess our sins, He is faithful and just to forgive us our sins, and to cleanse us from all unrighteousness (I John 1:9).

5. ***There is a sense in which believers will be ultimately and perfectly sanctified.***
   Thus sanctification in a believer is a past, accomplished fact, an ongoing process, and an ultimate, eternal state. Ultimate sanctification will be discussed later in this book in the category "the permanence of our salvation."

6. ***The Word of God is a very powerful agent in sanctification.***
   In referring to the church, Paul says:

   That He might sanctify and cleanse it with the washing of water *by the Word* (Ephesians 5:26).

7. ***Progressive sanctification involves both God's work and human effort.***
   Regarding God's work in sanctification, God is the initiator.

   For it is *God which worketh in you* both to will and to do of His good pleasure (Philippians 2:13).

Regarding the responsibility of man, we are to cleanse ourselves.

Having therefore these promises, dearly beloved, *let us cleanse ourselves* from all filthiness of the flesh and spirit, perfecting holiness in the fear of God (II Corinthians 7:1).

We are also given a number of admonitions. Here are a few:

Now *we exhort you,* brethren, warn them that are unruly, comfort the feeble-minded, support the weak, be patient toward all men. See that none render evil for evil unto any man; but ever follow that which is good, both among yourselves, and in all men, Rejoice evermore. Pray without ceasing. In every thing give thanks: for this is the will of God in Christ Jesus concerning you. Quench not the Spirit. Despise not prophesyings. Prove all things; hold fast that which is good. Abstain from all appearance of evil (I Thessalonians 5:14-22).

Notice that all these commands are from God and are not merely man-made!

This matter of obeying God is a *crucial* pursuit:

Follow peace with all men, and holiness, *without which no man shall see the Lord* (Hebrews 12:14).

8. ***A proper understanding and pursuit of sanctification surely influences lives.***
   Whether therefore ye eat, or drink, or whatsoever ye do, *do all to the glory of God* (I Corinthians 10:31).

   This pursuit should influence our attitudes toward God, worship, and every person God allows into our lives. God's Word has instructions on how believers ought to live, think, and act. In fact, there is a God-honoring approach to finances, education, every aspect of life.

Take time to be holy,
Speak oft with thy Lord;
Abide in Him always,
And feast on His Word.
Make friends of God's children,
Help those who are weak;
Forgetting in nothing
His blessing to seek.

Take time to be holy,
Be calm in thy soul;
Each thought and each motive
Beneath His control;
Thus led by His Spirit
To fountains of love,
Thou soon shalt be fitted
For service above.

Take Time to be Holy
William D. Longstaff

VII

Justification

And he believed in the Lord, and He counted it to him for righteousness
(Genesis 15:6).

The great German reformer Martin Luther grew up believing in the efficacy of the sacraments of Romanism. Before his conversion he was a Roman Catholic priest and the best-known attorney in all of Germany.

In his day the mass was held in Latin. Only the priesthood of the Church knew that language, so the people really did not understand what was happening in their houses of worship every Sunday. This is pretty much the way things were in much of the medieval world.

Then one day Luther read from the Scriptures how one is justified. The Holy Spirit moved mightily in his heart and he was saved. Thus justification is at the very heart of the Reformation movement and a major doctrine in our Biblical understanding of salvation today as well.

Listed below are some of the things Luther and others since him have taught from the Bible about the doctrine of justification.

1. ***It is an act of God whereby He declares all those who believe in Christ to be righteous.***

    Here is the picture we should get when we consider justification. We are in God's courtroom. Satan is our accuser, Jesus is our attorney, the Father is the judge. Having considered our case, that we have been saved and made holy through positional sanctification, the Father *declares* us to be righteous.

    Consider how magnificent such a truth as this is! God not only makes us holy, He legally DECLARES it! When God declares such, we can be sure that it is right and that no creature in all the universe can overturn such a decision!

    Being justified freely by His grace (Romans 3:24a).

    To declare, I say, at this time His righteousness: *that He might be just and the justifier* of him which believeth in Jesus (Romans 3:26).

    Therefore *being justified by faith,* we have peace with God through our Lord Jesus Christ (Romans 5:1).

2. ***It cannot be accomplished by keeping the Law or any of our "good works."***

For as many as are of the works of the Law are under the curse: for it is written, Cursed is every one that continueth not in all things which are written in the book to do them. But that *no man is justified by the Law in the sight of God,* It is evident: for, the just shall live by faith (Galatians 3:10-11).

3. *It causes a restoration to favor with God.*
    And the Scripture was fulfilled which saith, Abraham believed God, and it was imputed unto him for righteousness: and he was called *the friend of God* (James 2:23).

4. *It is taught in both the Old and New Testaments.*
    Blessed is the man *unto whom the Lord imputeth not iniquity,* and in whose spirit there is no guile (Psalm 32:2).

    That *being justified by His grace,* we should be made heirs according to the hope of eternal life (Titus 3:7).

5. *God keeps a record of it in the heavenly courts.*
    This is what the words "impute" and "reckon" mean when they are used in connection with justification.

    To wit, that God was in Christ, reconciling the world unto Himself, *not imputing their trespasses unto them;* and hath committed unto us the word of reconciliation (II Corinthians 5:19).

6. *It is by grace, faith, and the blood of Christ.*
    Being justified freely *by His grace...* (Romans 3:24).

    Therefore we conclude *that a man is justified by faith* without the deeds of the Law (Romans 3:28).

    Much more then, *being now justified by His blood,* we shall be saved from wrath through Him (Romans 5:9).

7. *Although it is a separate doctrine, it is related to sanctification.*
    In sanctification God makes a believer holy in position and practice. In justification God takes things one step farther. He actually, in a judicial sense, *declares* the believer to be holy and places the record in His court forever!

    Living, He loved me,   **One Day!**
    Dying, He saved me;   J. Wilbur
    Buried, He carried my sins far away;   Chapman
    Rising, He justified freely forever:
    One day He's coming—oh, glorious day!

VIII

Spirit Baptism

John truly baptized with water; but ye shall be baptized with the Holy Ghost not many days hence (Acts 1:5).

It is interesting to note the word "baptize" in the English and Greek languages. The early English translators did not have a word, so they *transliterated* the Greek verb *baptizo* into "baptize," thus creating a new word in English.

Various groups have differing ideas on what the verb *baptize* actually means, but a careful study of Greek literature, including the New Testament, reveals a bit of ambiguity. It is probably because of this ambiguity that the early English translators decided to invent a new word rather than take one position or another as to its exact meaning.

Note the different uses of the word in the references quoted below:

And when they were come from the market, except they wash, they eat not. And many other things there be, which they have received to hold, as the *washings* of cups, and pots, brazen vessels, and of tables (Mark 7:4).

John did baptize in the wilderness, and preach *the baptism of repentance* for the remission of sins (Mark 1:4).

Polybius (iii, 72) uses the verb to refer to soldiers *wading in water* during a military maneuver.

Josephus (in his *Jewish Wars*) uses this same verb to say that Jerusalem *was baptized* when the Roman legions under Titus destroyed the city in AD 70.

In addition to this, we sometimes use the word *baptism* today quite differently from a ceremonial ordinance conducted in a church by its officials. For instance, a sports announcer may speak of an athlete's *baptism,* his first action in that sport.

While there are some differences in the usage of the word *baptize* in Greek and English, there is also some controversy about what *Spirit baptism* is.

In certain circles of Christianity there are those who believe Spirit baptism is closely related to certain spiritual gifts, particularly speaking in tongues. Here is a typical presentation of such a position:

We believe full salvation comes with the baptism of the Holy Ghost with the initial evidence of speaking with other tongues. See the following verses:

But when they believed Philip preaching the things concerning the kingdom of God, and the name of Jesus Christ, *they were baptized,* both men and women. Then Simon himself believed also; and when he was baptized, he continued with Philip, and wondered, beholding the miracles and signs which were done. Now when the apostles which were at Jerusalem heard that Samaria had received the Word of God, they sent unto them Peter and John: Who, when they were come down, prayed for them, *that they might receive the Holy Ghost:* (For as yet He was fallen upon none of them: only they *were baptized in the name of the Lord Jesus*). Then laid they their hands on them, and they *received* the Holy Ghost (Acts 8:12-17).

Notice in this passage that there is mention of water baptism and *receiving* the Holy Spirit, but no reference is made to Spirit baptism or speaking in tongues. One has to "read in" such meaning from these verses in Acts to reach that conclusion.

While Peter yet spake these words, *the Holy Ghost fell on them which heard the Word.* And they of the circumcision which believed were astonished, as many as came with Peter, because that on the Gentiles also was poured out the *gift* of the Holy Ghost. For they heard them speak with tongues and magnify God (Acts 10:44-46).

Here we have speaking with tongues as an apparent result of "the gift of the Holy Ghost," but Spirit baptism is not mentioned. It is interesting to note that Peter commanded the new believers to be baptized *after* they had believed and spoken in tongues (verse 48).

Then said Paul, John verily baptized with the baptism of repentance, saying unto the people, that they should believe on Him which should come after him, that is, on Christ Jesus. And when Paul had laid his hands upon them, *the Holy Ghost came* on them; and they spake with other tongues and prophesied (Acts 19:4-6).

These verses indicate that water baptism was followed by a laying on of hands by Paul, a *coming* of the Holy Spirit, and a time of speaking in tongues and prophesying. The Holy Spirit "came on them," but there is no indication that this was a baptism of the Holy Spirit.

The simple truth is that none of these passages (or any other Scripture, for that matter) teach that Spirit baptism is the initiator of speaking in tongues. The role of tongues will be discussed later in this book.

There is another controversy about Spirit baptism that should be mentioned here. First, take a look at two verses from the Gospel of Luke:

John answered, saying unto them all, I indeed baptize you with water: but One mightier than I cometh, the latchet of whose shoes I am not worthy to unloose: He shall *baptize you with the Holy Ghost and with fire:* Whose fan is in His hand, and He will thoroughly purge His floor, and will gather the wheat into His garner; but the chaff He will burn with fire unquenchable (Luke 3:16-17).

Much is said about the phrase "and with fire." There are some who believe that Spirit baptism brings with it an extreme disposition of boldness, ostentatious behavior, and lack of self control, and they believe "and with fire" proves their point.

Look more closely at the remainder of this passage quoted above. It speaks of God's gathering His own together and also of His judgment of "the chaff." Such judgment will be *with fire unquenchable.* The point of this passage is clear. Spirit baptism is for believers; baptism with fire is the eternal punishment of unbelievers! Spirit baptism takes place at salvation; baptism by fire is an eschatological event.

Now let us consider the Biblical doctrine of Spirit baptism:

1. **Christ is involved in Spirit baptism.**
   I indeed have baptized you with water: *but He shall baptize you with the Holy Ghost* (Mark 1:8).

2. **Spirit baptism was prophesied by John the Baptist.**
   He *shall* baptize you with the Holy Ghost… (Matthew 3:11).

3. **I Corinthians 12:13 is the only verse that actually defines Spirit baptism.**
   For by one Spirit are we all baptized into one body, whether we be Jews or Gentiles, whether we be bond or free; and have been all made to drink into one body (I Corinthians 12:13).

   There are three key ideas in this verse:

   A. The verb "baptized" is in the aorist tense in the Greek. The main idea of this tense is *completed* action. In other words, those who are saved are Spirit baptized immediately at the time of their salvation. *It is an accomplished fact for all who believe.*

   B. The word "all" is important. There is no such thing as two different categories of believers, those who have been Spirit baptized and those who have not. The word "all" indicates clearly that *every* believer is Spirit baptized the moment he/she is saved.

   C. Notice the phrase "into one body" which is mentioned twice in this short verse.

   This is probably the most important concept to understand regarding Spirit baptism. The idea is clearly that of *initiation, at the moment of salvation, of all believers into the body of Christ.* All those who are saved by God's grace are related to one another because of Spirit baptism.

This body of believers goes by other names. Some call it the Church universal, some call it the Family of God, others use different terminology. The point, however, is very obvious: a believer is initiated into a spiritual body (along with all other believers) at the moment of salvation. This is the essence of Spirit baptism according to I Corinthians 12:13.

4. *Water baptism symbolizes Spirit baptism.*

Know ye not, that *as many as were baptized into Jesus Christ were baptized into His death?* Therefore we are buried with Him by baptism into death: that like as Christ was raised up from the dead by the glory of the Father, even so we also should walk in newness of life (Romans 6:3-4).

The Church's One Foundation
Samuel J. Stone

The Church's one foundation
Is Jesus Christ, her Lord;
She is His new creation,
By water and the Word;
From heaven He came and bought her
To be His holy bride;
With His own blood He bought her,
And for her life He died!

IX

Adoption

For ye are all the children of God by faith in Jesus Christ (Galatians 3:26).

In the last chapter we saw that a believer is Spirit baptized into the Church the moment he is saved. We might well say that Spirit baptism is his initiation into that body.

In this chapter we will see that God wants His relationship with His own to be much closer than just a mere initiation. He *adopts* us into His family and grants to us many privileges with such a relationship. Consider where we were before we were saved!

In our natural state we have the Devil as our father:
Ye are of your father, *the devil,* and the lusts of your father ye will do (John 8:44).

Once we have been made a new creature in Christ and brought into God's family, we can claim God as our Father. The Fatherhood of God, however, is only for those who have placed their faith in His Son Jesus Christ (reread John 8:44 above, referring to unbelievers).

That having been said, what does the Bible say about our being adopted into the family of God?

1. **God loves us as dear children.**
    But as many as received Him, to them gave He the power to become *the sons of God,* even to them that believe on His name (John 1:12).

    The word "sons" here is *teknon* in the Greek and means "young children."

2. **This new relationship eliminates fear.**
    For as many as are led by the Spirit of God, they are the sons of God. For ye *have not received the spirit of bondage again to fear;* but ye have received the Spirit of adoption, whereby we cry, Abba, Father (Romans 8:14-15).

    The word "Abba" is Aramaic and is generally the first simple word that an infant in a middle eastern culture speaks when referring to his father. It is clearly a term of trust and endearment.

3. **Somehow adoption is connected to the new bodies we'll receive in heaven.**
    For we know that the whole creation groaneth and travaileth in pain together until now. And not only they, but ourselves also, which have the firstfruits of the Spirit, even we ourselves groan within ourselves, *waiting for the adoption,* to wit, the redemption of our body (Romans 8:22-23).

For we are saved by hope: but hope that is seen is not hope; for what a man seeth, why doth he yet hope for? But if we hope for that we see not, then do we *with patience wait for it* (Romans 8:24-25).

4. ***Adoption was God's choice.***
Having predestinated us *unto the adoption of children* by Jesus Christ to Himself, according to *the good pleasure of His will* (Ephesians 1:5).

5. ***This adoption brings very significant privileges to us even in this life.***
But when the fullness of the time was come, God sent forth His Son, made of a woman, made under the Law, To redeem them that were under the Law, that we might receive the adoption of sons. And because ye are sons, God hath sent forth the Spirit of His Son into your hearts, crying, Abba, Father. Wherefore *thou art no more a servant, but a son; and if so, then an heir of God* through Christ (Galatians 4:4-6).

There is a very significant idea in these verses.

The word translated "sons" is from the Greek noun *hwios*. This particular word indicates a fully adult son who has all the rights and privileges his father can bestow. If a father leaves something to a son in his final will and testament, he may very well include a statement that his son is entitled to what he has bestowed upon him, but that the son will have access to all these things *when he turns a certain age.* The father may stipulate an age of eighteen or twenty-one or some other age.

The point is, when we are adopted into God's family, we have both the special attachment of very young children (*teknon*) but also the special privileges of a fully adult son, including heirship!

The Spirit Himself beareth witness with our Spirit, that we are the children of God: And if children, then *heirs; heirs of God, and joint heirs with Christ* (Romans 8:16-17a).

6. ***By faith we are delivered from the Law's curse when we are adopted by God.***
Wherefore the Law was our schoolmaster to bring us unto Christ, that we might be justified by faith. But after that faith is come, *we are no longer under a school-master. For ye are all children of God by faith in Christ Jesus* (Galatians 3:24-26).

A Child of the King
Harriett Buell

I once was an outcast
Stranger on earth,
A sinner by choice,
And an alien by birth,
But I've been adopted,
My name's written down,
An heir of salvation,
The kingdom and crown!

I'm a child of the King,
A child of the king;
With Jesus my Savior,
I'm a child of the King!

X

Priesthood

But ye are a chosen generation, a royal priesthood, an holy nation, a peculiar people; that ye should show forth the praises of Him Who hath called you out of darkness into His marvelous light (I Peter 2:9).

The Old Testament office of priesthood begins shortly after the exodus and is described in considerable detail in Exodus 28-29 and Leviticus 8. The children of Israel were to confess their sins to a priest, and the priest was to pray for the people, offering sacrifices on their behalf.

We will offer a short list of the duties of Old Testament priests here:

1. To offer sacrifices (Leviticus 1:4-17).
2. To pronounce benedictions (Numbers 6:22-27).
3. To teach the Law (Leviticus 10:11).
4. To keep the sacred fire always burning (Leviticus 6:12-13).
5. To supervise the tithing (Nehemiah 4:5-15).
6. To be responsible for the sanctuary (Numbers 4:5-15).
7. To value things devoted (Leviticus 27:8-12).

These priests should be contrasted with Old Testament prophets. A *priest* listened to the confessions and needs of the people and presented all these burdens to God. In other words, the priest ministered as a mediator. On the other hand, a *prophet* received a message from God and presented it to the people. A priest dealt with sacrifices often; a prophet proclaimed God's plan often.

It was a cumbersome system, but the real message was that forgiveness came by repentance, blood sacrifices, faith, and God's grace. The New Testament, however, brought a better way to do these things:

But now hath He obtained a more excellent ministry, by how much also *He is the mediator of a better covenant, which was established upon better promises* (Hebrews 8:6).

So how is the New Testament arrangement better?

1. Whereas an Old Testament priest had to offer sacrifices continually, *Jesus Christ offered Himself once for all our sin.*

    For every high priest taken from among men is ordained for men in things pertaining to God, that he may offer both *gifts and sacrifices for sins:* Who can have compassion on the ignorant, and on them that are out of the way; for that he himself also is compassed with infirmity. And by reason hereof, he ought, as for the people, so also for himself, to offer for sins (Hebrews 5:1-3).

So Christ was *once* offered to bear the sins of many; and unto them which look for Him shall He appear the second time without sin unto salvation (Hebrews 9:28).

2. An Old Testament priest listened to the sins of the people, but now we can confess our sin directly to God. This is a great privilege that believers should practice every time they stumble into sin. Failure to do so results in a loss of fellowship with God.

If we *confess* our sins, He is faithful and just to forgive us our sins, and to cleanse us from all unrighteousness (I John 1:9).

"Confession" involves taking the same attitude toward sin that God does.

3. Whereas an Old Testament priest prayed for the people, believers today can go directly to God in prayer.

Jesus taught direct prayer (rather than through a priest) in His sermon on the mount:

After this manner pray ye: *Our Father which art in heaven...* (Matthew 6:9).

4. Our prayer is to be multi-faceted, personal, and sincere, even for our own needs:

Give us this day our daily bread (Matthew 6:11).

Casting all your care upon Him; for He careth for you (I Peter 5:7).

5. We are to pray constantly.

Pray without ceasing (I Thessalonians 5:17).

6. We are actually our own priests before God.

John to the seven churches which are in Asia; Grace be unto you, and peace, from Him which is, and which was, and which is to come; and from the seven spirits which are before His throne; And from Jesus Christ, Who is the faithful witness, and the first begotten of the dead, and the prince of the kings of the earth, Unto Him that loved us, and washed us from our sins in His own blood, And *hath made us kings and priests unto God and His Father;* to Him be glory for ever and ever. Amen (Revelation 1:4-6).

7. Whereas high priests used to be humans, Christ is now our only Mediator.

For there is one God, *and one mediator between God and men, the man Christ Jesus* (I Timothy 2:5).

I pray for them; I pray not for the world, but for them which Thou hast given Me; for they are Thine (John 17:9).

It is significant also to note that the Holy Spirit also intercedes for believers as well:

Likewise the Spirit also helpeth our infirmities: for we know not what we should pray for as we ought: but the Spirit itself *maketh intercession for us* with groanings which cannot be uttered (Romans 8:26).

Our great High Priest is sitting *At God's right hand above,* *For us His hands uplifting* *In sympathy and love:* *Whilst here below in weakness,* *We onward speed our way,* *In sorrow oft and sickness,* *We sigh, and groan, and pray.*	**Our Great High Priest is Sitting** A.P. Cecil

Sweet hour of prayer! *Sweet hour of prayer!* *That calls me from a world of care,* *And bids me at my Father's throne,* *Make all my wants and wishes known.* *In seasons of distress and grief* *My soul has often found relief;* *And oft escaped the tempter's snare,* *By thy return, sweet hour of prayer!*	**Sweet Hour of Prayer** W.W. Walford

XI

Ambassadorship

For which I am an ambassador in bonds: that therein I may speak boldly, as I ought to speak (Ephesians 6:20).

Today virtually every country in the world has people who represent their government to other countries. These people are called ambassadors. Obviously, they have a position of some importance, although they seldom actually make significant governmental policies.

The Apostle Paul speaks of himself and believers in general as ambassadors for Christ. This is a position which God grants to believers so they have an opportunity to serve and represent their Savior.

We can see what the Bible says about ambassadors by considering these following points:

1. The Greek verb "to be an ambassador" is *presbeuo.* This word is found both in the Septuagint (the Greek translation of the Old Testament done before the time of Christ) and the New Testament. Its most common meanings are "to be an elder, to take precedence, to be an ambassador." The word connotes respect, authority, maturity, and responsibility.

2. Being an ambassador or "representative" was fairly commonplace even in early Old Testament times. Below are two references in which Moses attempts to make contact with leaders of two foreign countries for a right of passage after the exodus:

   And Moses sent *messengers* from Kadesh unto the king of Edom, Thus saith thy brother Israel, Thou knowest all the travail that hath befallen us: How our fathers went down into Egypt, and we have dwelt in Egypt a long time; and the Egyptians vexed us, and our fathers: And when we cried unto the Lord, He heard our voice, and sent an angel, and hath brought us forth out of Egypt: and behold, we are in Kadesh, a city in the uttermost of thy border: Let us pass, I pray thee, through thy country (Numbers 20:14-17a).

   And Israel sent *messengers* unto Sihon king of the Amorites, saying, Let me pass through thy land... (Numbers 21:21-22a).

3. A competent representative is a very good thing.

   A faithful ambassador *is health* (Proverbs 13:17b).

4. A poor representative can be a very bad thing.

A *wicked messenger falleth into mischief* (Proverbs 13:17a).

Now we must look at what Paul says about the Christian and his position as an ambassador. His thoughts are summarized in passages in his epistle to the Ephesians (also in II Corinthians and Romans).

For which cause *I am an ambassador* in bonds (Ephesians 6:20).

Now then *we are ambassadors for Christ,* as though God did beseech you by us: we pray you in Christ's stead, be ye reconciled to God (II Corinthians 5:20).

We see five important aspects of our ambassadorship in the New Testament:

1. **It should be done by Christians even under dire circumstances.**
   Paul speaks of being "in bonds" (in prison) in Ephesians 6:20. He considered it important to maintain a good testimony and to be a good representative, even in those unpleasant conditions.

2. **An ambassador should speak boldly.**
   "…that *therein I may speak boldly, as I ought to speak*" (Ephesians 6:20b). It was important that the Apostle Paul speak up clearly and confidently in the hostile environment of his day. As an Apostle it was his duty to do so. As ambassadors of the same Savior, we must be bold in our testimony as well!

3. **We are ambassadors for Christ.**
   "Now then *we are ambassadors for Christ*" (II Corinthians 5:20). It would be a significant thing to be a representative of our own country in a foreign land, but those who are Christians represent the Son of God wherever they go! We have a great commission to fulfill!

4. **Our message is urgent.**
   "…*as though God did beseech you by us*" (II Corinthians 5:20). We should never take our salvation or our position in Christ lightly. In addition, God has given us this great opportunity and responsibility. What we say and how we say it is very important!

5. **Our ultimate goal is to present the Gospel.**
   How then shall they call on Him in Whom they have not believed? And how shall they believe in Him of Whom they have not heard? And how shall they hear without a preacher? *And how shall they preach, except they be sent...* (Romans 10:14-15a)?

In the last two chapters we have seen that God in His love and wisdom has given all believers two very important positions: a priesthood and an ambassadorship. We are to pray for others, to represent Christ to a sinful world, and to maintain a good testimony in both ministries. These facts should humble us and cause us to be very careful to honor our Savior by our appearance, conduct, and attitude.

A charge to keep I have,
A God to glorify.
A never-dying soul to save,
And fit it for the sky.

To serve the present age,
My calling to fulfill;
O may it all my powers engage,
To do my Master's will!

A Charge to Keep I Have
Charles Wesley

XII

Indwelling of the Holy Spirit

Know ye not that ye are the temple of God, and that the Spirit of God dwelleth in you (I Corinthians 3:16)?

Having read the last two chapters, one may wonder how believers can possibly be successful in fulfilling such demanding ministries as a priesthood and an ambassadorship. After all, we are humans who have many limitations. In addition to that, we are fallen creatures who have a sinful nature always with us.

The truth be told, if we had to do these things in our own strength or ingenuity, we would fail miserably. God, however, has sent His Holy Spirit to indwell us.

The Holy Spirit is very active in the life of a believer!

1. ***Jesus prophesied that the Holy Spirit would indwell believers.***
   And I will pray the Father, *and He shall give you another Comforter,* that He may abide with you for ever. Even the Spirit of truth; Whom the world cannot receive, because it seeth Him not, neither knoweth Him; for *He dwelleth with you, and shall be in you* (John 14:16-17).

   Notice "Whom the world cannot receive." The Holy Spirit does not indwell unbelievers because they do not know Him or our Savior!

2. ***All believers possess the Holy Spirit.***
   But ye are not in the flesh, but in the Spirit, if so be that the Spirit of God dwell in you. Now *if any man have not the Spirit of Christ, he is none of His* (Romans 8:9).

   What? Know ye not that *your body is the temple of the Holy Ghost which is in you,* which ye have of God, and ye are not your own (I Corinthians 6:19)?

It is important to note the Greek noun translated "temple" in I Corinthians 6:19 (quoted above). This word refers to the innermost sanctuary of the temple where only high priests could enter in Old Testament times. Our physical bodies are so important to God that He treats them a place where His Holy Spirit continually dwells, and He insists that His temple be kept clean!

3. ***The Holy Spirit is involved in many aspects of our salvation.***
   We have already seen that He is heavily involved in regeneration, Spirit baptism, and sanctification. Actually, as we shall see, He does much more!

4. ***His indwelling ministry is multi-faceted.***

A. We can walk and live with Him.
    If we *live* in the Spirit, *let us also walk* in the Spirit (Galatians 5:25).

B. He disciplines when the occasion calls for it.
    But a certain man named Ananias, with Sapphira his wife, sold a possession,
    And kept back part of the price, his wife also being privy to it, and brought
    a certain part, and laid it at the apostle's feet. But Peter said, Ananias, why
    hath Satan filled thine heart *to lie to the Holy Ghost,* and to keep back part of
    the price of the land? Whiles it remained, was it not thine own? And after it
    was sold, was it not in thine own power? Why hast thou conceived this
    thing in thine heart? Thou hast not lied unto men, but unto God. *And
    Ananias, hearing these words fell down, and gave up the ghost:* and great
    fear came on all them that heard these things (Acts 5:1-5).

C. He gives direction to those who face uncertain circumstances.
    And the angel of the Lord spake unto Philip, saying, Arise, and go toward
    the south unto the way that goeth down from Jerusalem unto Gaza, which is
    desert. And he arose and went: and, behold, a man of Ethiopia, an eunich of
    great authority under Candace queen of the Ethiopians, who had the charge
    of all her treasure, and had come to Jerusalem for to worship, Was
    returning, and sitting in his chariot read Esaias the prophet. *Then the Spirit
    said unto Philip, Go near, and join thyself to this chariot* (Acts 8:26-29).

D. He makes appointments.
    As they ministered to the Lord, and fasted, *the Holy Ghost said, Separate
    me Barnabas and Saul for the work whereunto I have called them.* And
    when they had...prayed... they laid their hands on them... (Acts 13:2-3).

E. He sometimes prohibits certain activities, even though they may seem
    good.
    Now when they had gone throughout Phrygia and the region of Galatia,
    and *were forbidden of the Holy Ghost to preach the Word in Asia,* After
    they were come to Mysia, they assayed to go into Bithynia: but *the Spirit
    suffered them not* (Acts 16:6-7).

F. He gives wisdom when making decisions.
    In Acts 15 the Apostles held a council in Jerusalem. The issue
    under discussion was whether or not the Gospel was intended to save
    Gentiles. The answer, of course, was that the message of salvation is
    for all. The question then came up whether or not it was wise to make
    Gentiles become Jews or keep their traditions after being saved.

    For *it seemed good to the Holy Ghost, and to us,* to lay upon you no
    greater burden than these necessary things: That ye abstain from
    meats offered to idols, and from blood, and from things strangled, and

from fornicaton: which if ye keep yourselves, ye shall do well. Fare ye well (Acts 15:28-29).

G. He gives believers the ability to get victory over sin.
    For if ye live after the flesh, ye shall die: but *if ye through the Spirit do mortify the deeds of the body,* ye shall live (Romans 8:13).

    This I say then, *Walk in the Spirit, and ye shall not fulfill the lust of the flesh* (Galatians 5:16).

H. He convicts of sin.
    Nevertheless I tell you the truth; It is expedient for you that I go away: for if I go not away, the Comforter will not come unto you; but if I depart, I will send Him unto you. And when He comes, *He will reprove the world of sin,* and of righteousness, and of judgment: Of sin because they believe not on Me; Of righteousness, because I go to My Father, and ye see Me no more; Of judgment, because the prince of this world is judged (John 16:7-11).

I. He teaches.
    These things have I spoken unto you, being yet present with you. But the Comforter, which is the Holy Ghost, Whom the Father will send in My name, *He shall teach you all things,* and bring all things to your remembrance, whatsoever I have said unto you (John 14:25-26).

    Howbeit when He, the Spirit of truth, is come, *He will guide you into all truth:* For He shall not speak of Himself: but whatsoever He shall hear, that shall He speak: and He will show you things to come (John16:13).

    Now we have received not the spirit of the world, but the Spirit which is of God; *that we might know the things that are freely given to us of God.* Which things also we speak, not in the words which man's wisdom teacheth, but which the Holy Ghost teacheth; comparing spiritual things with spiritual (I Corinthians 2:12-13).

    So Who is this Holy Spirit Who indwells the believer from the moment of his salvation? Of course He is God, the third Person of the trinity, but what kind of Person is He? There are some who seem to think He causes believers to do rather strange things, but below are listed the characteristics which the Scriptures reveal about Him:

1. He is very caring.
    Reread John 14:26; 16:7. There are many Scriptures which teach this great truth. Here is another:
    Let not your heart be troubled, neither let it be afraid (John 14:27).

2. He is very peaceful (as shown at our Lord's baptism).
   And it came to pass in those days, that Jesus came from Nazareth of Galilee, and was baptized of John in Jordan. And straightway coming up out of the water, He saw the heavens opened, *and the Spirit of God descending upon Him* (Mark 1:9-10).

3. He is not ostentatious, giving glory to the Son, not Himself. In speaking about the Holy Spirit, our Lord said, *"He shall glorify Me:* for He shall receive of Mine, and shall show it unto you" (John 16:14).

4. He is sensitive and can be grieved.
   But they rebelled and vexed His Holy Spirit: therefore he was turned to be their enemy, and he fought against them (Isaiah 63:10).

   And grieve not the Holy Spirit of God, whereby ye are sealed unto the day of redemption (Ephesians 4:30).

5. He is sensitive and can be lied to.
   But Peter said, Ananias, *why hath Satan filled thine heart to lie to the Holy Ghost* (Acts 5:3)?

6. He is sensitive and can be insulted.
   Of how much sorer punishment, suppose ye, shall he be thought worthy, who hath trodden under foot the Son of God, and hath counted the blood of the covenant, wherewith he was sanctified, an unholy thing, *and hath done despite to the Spirit of grace* (Hebrews 10:29)?

7. He is sensitive and can be resisted.
   Ye stiffnecked and uncircumcised in heart and ears, *ye do always resist the Holy Ghost:* as your fathers did, so do ye (Acts 7:51).

8. He is sensitive and can be blasphemed.
   Wherefore I say unto you, All manner of sin and blasphemy shall be forgiven unto men: *but the blasphemy against the Holy Ghost shall not be forgiven* unto men (Matthew 12:31).

And so we see from Scripture that the Holy Spirit Who indwells the believer is caring, peaceful, not loud, and quite sensitive. He will not force us into things, but His ministry is to quietly urge the believer to yield to Him.

These verses concerning Elijah are typical of how the Holy Spirit operates.

And He said, Go forth, and stand upon the mount before the Lord. And, behold the Lord passed by, and a great and strong wind rent the mountains, and brake in pieces the rocks before the Lord: but the Lord was not in the wind:

and after the wind an earthquake; but the Lord was not in the earthquake: And after the earthquake a fire; but the Lord was not in the fire: *and after the fire a still small voice* (I Kings 19:11-12).

One last thought about this subject. Many teach/preach that Christians should "dedicate" themselves to the ministry of the Holy Spirit. On the surface this sounds like a good thing, but actually it is rather inadequate. "Unconditional surrender" is much more fitting. It is possible to be dedicated to something *you want to do,* but in unconditional surrender a believer totally allows the Holy Spirit to dominate in every aspect of life.

I beseech you therefore, by the mercies of God, *that ye present your bodies a living sacrifice,* holy, acceptable unto God, which is your reasonable service. And be not conformed to this world: but be ye transformed by the renewing of your mind, that ye may prove what is that good, and acceptable, and perfect will of God (Roman 12:1-2; see also Galatians 2:20).

Holy Ghost with light Divine,
Dwelling in this heart of mine;
Take all doubts and fears away,
As I tread the narrow way.

Holy Ghost with pow'r Divine,
Strengthen this weak heart of mine;
When my prayers I can't express
Thou dost aid in my distress.

Holy Ghost with
Light Divine
Andrew Reed

XIII

Filling of the Holy Spirit

And be not drunk with wine, wherein is excess; but be filled with the Spirit (Ephesians 5:18).

We have seen thus far that Spirit baptism, positional sanctification, and regeneration are works of the Holy Spirit that are accomplished at the very moment of salvation.

There is another ministry of the Holy Spirit, however, which is not automatic. Ephesians 5:18 *commands* us to be filled with the Holy Spirit rather than telling us that He fills us. In other words, we have a responsibility to allow Him to fill us.

The wine mentioned in Ephesians 5:18 has a way of controlling lives if the one drinking it allows it to have such dominance. Obviously a drunken stupor is something which does not honor God or allow the believer to be effective in service to the Lord. Being filled with the Holy Spirit and allowing Him to control our lives, however, produces wonderful results.

One good way to describe the filling of the Holy Spirit would be to say that we do not get more of Him (He already indwells the believer at salvation), but He gets all of us.

He does not force Himself into every aspect of our lives because He is gentlemanly and sensitive. He quietly works in such a way that we need to be very aware of His will and ways. It is when we totally surrender to Him that we are filled with Him and enjoy great blessings as a result. It should be emphasized that the Holy Spirit is very sensitive and will not force His way into various aspects of our lives: we must let Him be our controller if He is to fill us.

It should also be emphasized here that there is a distinction between the *indwelling* of the Holy Spirit and the *filling* of the Holy Spirit. In His indwelling ministry He teaches, guides, convicts, and does other things. This is an automatic aspect of our salvation, and the Holy Spirit indwells from the moment we are saved.

In His ministry of filling, He takes control of every aspect of our lives. This is not an automatic transaction at the moment of salvation. This is something that a believer must decide to allow after he/she has been saved.

We do well to consider four passages to see what the Scriptures teach about the filling of the Spirit. The first of these is found in Ephesians 5:18:

And be not drunk with wine, wherein is excess: *but be filled with the Spirit.*

This discussion continues through Ephesians 6:9. Here are the highlights:

1. ***The believer has a song in his heart when he is filled with the Holy Spirit.***
    Speaking to yourselves in psalms and hymns and spiritual songs, singing and making melody in your heart to the Lord; Giving thanks always for all things unto God and the Father… (Ephesians 5:19-20).

2. ***The believer has a submissive attitude when he is filled with the Holy Spirit.***
    Submitting yourselves one to another in the fear of God (Ephesians 5:21).

3. ***Marriages work as they should when a couple is filled with the Holy Spirit.***
    Regarding wives, the Scriptures say,

    Wives, *submit yourselves unto your own husbands,* as unto the Lord (Ephesians 5:22).

    Of course, this does not in any way make the wife a "second class citizen," neither does it make her opinion irrelevant. It has been the observation of many that wives who are Spirit-filled and submissive are extremely happy, just as Ephesians 5:19-20 indicates. The Holy Spirit is especially concerned with the marriages of believers.

    Regarding husbands, the Scriptures say,

    Husbands, *love your wives, even as Christ also loved the church,* and gave Himself for it (Ephesians 5:25).

    Obviously, this is a very significant commitment that can only be fulfilled when a man has totally yielded control of his life and marriage to the Spirit's control. The discussion of a man's love for his wife continues through Ephesians 5:33.

4. ***Children and parents get along well when all are filled with the Holy Spirit.***
    Children, *obey your parents in the Lord: for this is right.* Honor thy father and mother; which is the first commandment with promise; That it may be well with thee, and thou mayest live long on the earth (Ephesians 6:1-3).

5. ***Fathers have a good attitude toward their children when they are Spirit-filled.***
    And ye fathers, *provoke not your children to wrath:* but bring them up in the nurture and admonition of the Lord (Ephesians 6:4).

6. ***Servants have a good relationship with masters when they are Spirit-filled.***
    The closest equivalent we have today is the employer/employee relationship many have in their places of work. Notice how the Apostle Paul approaches this matter:

    Servants, be obedient to them that are your masters according to the flesh, with fear and trembling, In singleness of your heart, as unto Christ; Not with eyeservice, as menpleasers; but as the servant of Christ, doing the will of God from the heart (Ephesians 6:5-6).

The discussion about servants continues through verse 8 of this chapter.

7. ***Masters have a good relationship with servants when they are Spirit-filled.***
And ye masters, *do the same unto them, forbearing threatening:* knowing that your Master also is in heaven; neither is there respect of persons with Him (Ephesians 6:9).

Thus we see that a Spirit-filled believer enjoys good relationships in all aspects of his life. God's plan is that Christians enjoy their walk with Him!

I am come that they might have life, and that they might have it more abundantly (John 10:10b).

The second passage is Acts 4:31-32:

And when they had prayed, the place was shaken where they were assembled together; *and they were filled with the Holy Ghost,* and they spake the Word of God with boldness. And the multitude of them which believed were of one heart and of one soul....

The most obvious result of being filled with the Holy Spirit in this passage is *unity* (they were of one heart and one soul).

The third passage is Acts 13:8-12:

But Elymas the sorcerer (for so is his name by interpretation) withstood them, seeking to turn away the deputy from the faith. Then Saul (who is also called Paul), *filled with the Holy Ghost,* set his eyes on him, And said, O full of subtlety and all mischief, thou child of the devil, thou enemy of righteousness, wilt thou not cease to pervert the right ways of the Lord? And now, behold, the hand of the Lord is upon thee, and thou shalt be blind, not seeing the sun for a season. And immediately there fell on him a mist and a darkness; and he went about seeking some to lead him by the hand. Then the deputy, when he saw what was done, believed, being astonished at the doctrine of the Lord.

We see three results of being filled with the Holy Spirit from this passage:

1. *Discernment.* Paul was able to see and react to the wicked ways of Elymas very quickly.

2. *A miracle.* Paul, through the power of the Holy Spirit, was able to predict the blindness of the sorcerer.

3. *Salvation.* The deputy believed, even though Elymas did all he could to stop Him from believing.

The fourth passage is found in Acts 4:1-20. The Scriptures reveal in verse 8 that Peter was "filled with the Holy Ghost." What were the results?

1. *Evangelism on a grand scale.*
Howbeit many of them which heard the Word believed; *and the number of the men was about five thousand* (Acts 4:4).

2. *Boldness to preach and serve the Lord.*
Now *when they saw the boldness of Peter and John,* and perceived that they were unlearned and ignorant men, they marveled; and they took knowledge of them, that they had been with Jesus. And beholding the man which was healed standing with them, they could say nothing against it (Acts 4:13-14).

A few things should be said in conclusion. The *command* to be filled with the Holy Spirit is in the present tense in the Greek. The main idea is that it should be a *continual* state. Believers should be always yielding to His control, not just occasionally or in some insincere way.

The world certainly does not understand a truth like this! Their general attitude is that each has "rights," and nobody (not even the Holy Spirit) should tell anyone what to do, what to be, or what to believe. This attitude, of course, is basically rebellion and produces discord, heartache, and a lack of spiritual discernment among other poor results.

The Spirit-filled Christian knows better and lives his life for the glory of his Savior in the power and joy of the Holy Spirit.

Have Thine own way, Lord!
Have Thine own way!
Thou art the potter,
I am the clay.
Mould me and make me
After Thy will,
While I am waiting,
Yielded and still.

Have Thine own way, Lord!
Have Thine own way!
Search me and try me,
Master today!
Whiter than snow, Lord,
Wash me just now,
As in Thy presence,
Humbly I bow.

Have Thine own way, Lord!
Have Thine own way!
Wounded and weary,
Help me, I pray!
Power—all power—
Surely is Thine!
Touch me and heal me,
Savior Divine!

Have Thine own way, Lord!
Have Thine own way!
Hold o'er my being
Absolute sway!
Fill with Thy Spirit
Till all shall see
Christ only, always,
Living in me!

Have Thine Own Way, Lord!
Adelaide A. Pollard

XIV

Spiritual Gifts

But all these worketh that one and the selfsame Spirit, dividing to every man severally as He will (I Corinthians 12:11).

Many in the church today feel they are inadequate to serve the Lord because they feel they are not good speakers, do not have experience in a leadership role, or can only make a "joyful noise" unto the Lord rather than singing with confidence. In fact this "problem" has existed for thousands of years!

Even Moses, the great leader God used to bring the children of Israel out of Egyptian bondage, felt inadequate to do the work God gave him to do. Here is what Moses said to Him:

And Moses answered and said, But, behold, *they will not believe me,* nor hearken unto my voice: for they will say, The Lord hath not appeared unto thee (Exodus 4:1).

God, however, had other things than "excuse making" for Moses!

And He said, *Certainly I will be with thee;* and this shall be a token unto thee, that I have sent thee: When thou hast brought forth the people out of Egypt, ye shall serve God upon this mountain (Exodus 3:12).

In another context God offers Moses even more:

And the Lord said unto him, *What is that in thine hand? And he said, A rod. And He said, Cast it on the ground. And he cast it on the ground, and it became a serpent...* (Exodus 4:2-3).

We know that God gave all the miracles, confidence, assistance, and opportunities that Moses needed in order to be effective in service. The same can be said for every believer today! How does God accomplish this goal? There are primarily two ministries of the Holy Spirit that make all the difference: spiritual gifts and the fruit of the Spirit. These two subjects will be the focus of the next two chapters.

This chapter will deal with the subject of spiritual gifts. The Greek noun *charis* is normally translated "grace," whereas the noun *charisma* is normally translated "gift." Simply put, a gift from God is one of the results of His grace. This is true in the gift of eternal life that He offers and also the spiritual gifts He provides for those who have trusted in Him.

So what does the Bible have to say about spiritual gifts? Below is a list of clearly revealed truth:

1. ***Ignorance about spiritual gifts is not a virtue.***
    Now concerning spiritual gifts, brethren, *I would not have you ignorant* (I Corinthians 12:1).

2. ***Spiritual gifts are given as He wills, not as believers seek or pray.***
    But all these worketh that one and the selfsame Spirit, dividing to every man severally *as He will* (I Corinthians 12:11).

    But now hath God set the members every one of them in the body, *as it hath pleased Him.* And if they were all one member, where were the body (I Corinthians 12:18-19)?

    How shall we escape if we neglect so great salvation; which at the first began to be spoken by the Lord, and was confirmed unto us by them that heard Him; God also bearing them witness, both with signs and wonders, and with divers miracles *and gifts of the Holy Ghost, according to His own will* (Hebrews 2:3-4)?

3. ***All spiritual gifts are from the same source.***
    Now there are diversities of gifts, *but the same Spirit.* And there are diversities of administrations, *but it is the same Lord.* And there are diversities of operations, *but it is the same God which worketh all in all* (I Corinthians 12:4-6).

4. ***Every gift is for the benefit of the Lord's work.***
    But the manifestation of the Spirit is given to every man *to profit withal* (I Corinthians 12:7).

5. ***Every believer has at least one spiritual gift.***
    …but it is the same *God which worketh all in all* (I Corinthians 12:6b).

    …dividing *to every man severally…* (I Corinthians 12:11b).

6. ***Gifts are to bring unity, not confusion and arrogance.***
    For as the body is one, and hath many members, and all the members of that one body, *being many, are one body:* so also is Christ (I Corinthians 12:12; read also I Corinthians 12:14-27).

    That there should be no schism in the body; but that the members should have the same care one for another (I Corinthians 12:25).

7. ***As valuable as spiritual gifts are, there is a "more excellent way."***
    …and yet show I unto you *a more excellent way* (I Corinthians 12:31).

What is the "more excellent way"? Quite obviously the answer is to be found in the next chapter, I Corinthians 13, the great love chapter. Spiritual gifts without love are useless. In fact, *anything* done without love does not benefit anybody! This is the all important point of I Corinthians 13:1-3:

> Though I speak with the tongues of men and of angels, and have not charity, *I am become as sounding brass, or a tinkling cymbal.* And though I have the gift of prophecy, and understand all mysteries, and all knowledge; and though I have all faith, So that I could remove mountains, and have not charity, *I am nothing.* And though I bestow all my goods to feed the poor, and though I give my body to be burned, and have not charity, *it profiteth me nothing.*

In addition, spiritual gifts are temporal in nature, but love is eternal. This is clearly one of the greatest spiritual truths in all the Word of God!

> *Charity never faileth;* but whether there be prophecies, they shall fail; whether there be tongues, they shall cease; whether there be knowledge, it shall vanish away (I Corinthians 13:8).

> *And now abideth faith, hope, charity,* these three; but the greatest of these is charity (I Corinthians 13:13).

8.   ***The gift of tongues is regulated.***
The entire 14th chapter of I Corinthians is devoted to explaining potential abuses about the gift of tongues. In addition, several regulations are laid out by the Apostle Paul in this chapter (14:13, 26-30, 32, 34, 39-40).

It is significant to note that when the fruit of the Spirit is discussed in Galatians 5, Paul points out

> ...*against such there is no law* (Galatians 5:23b).

9.   ***Not all have the same spiritual gifts.***
Are all apostles? Are all prophets? Are all teachers? Are all workers of miracles? *Have all the gifts of healing? Do all speak with tongues? Do all interpret* (I Corinthians 12:29-30)?

It is significant to recognize what is happening in the Greek of these two verses. All the questions asked expect a very definite "no" response. The clear implication is that not all believers have the same spiritual gifts. God's Church would certainly lack effectiveness if such were the case!

10.   ***Claims to have spiritual gifts should be tested by doctrine.***
Ye know that ye were Gentiles, carried away unto these dumb idols, even as ye were led. Wherefore I give you to understand, *that no man speaking by the Spirit of God calleth Jesus accursed: and that no man can say Jesus is the Lord, but by the Holy Ghost* (I Corinthians 12:2-3).

11. ***Spiritual gifts have significance, but they also have limitations.***
For we know in part, and we prophesy in part (I Corinthians 13:9; read also 13: 10-12).

The passages in Scripture which mention the various spiritual gifts are I Corinthians 12 and Romans 12. Here is a listing:

I Corinthians 12:8	wisdom, knowledge
I Corinthians 12:9	faith, healing
I Corinthians 12:10	miracles, prophecy, discernment, tongues, interpretation
I Corinthians 12:28	apostles, prophets, teachers, miracles, helps, government
Romans 12:7	ministry
Romans 12:8	exhorting, giving, ruling, mercy

Every Christian can *try* to serve God in virtually any ministry imaginable, but it is only when God has given a gift specifically suited for a particular kind of service that he/she will be successful. Trying to serve the Lord without the gift to do it is like trying to build an airplane without any knowledge of science, mathematics, or mechanics!

On the other hand, *because God has given every believer at least one spiritual gift,* there really is no excuse for not serving Him! He has given His own a supernatural ability to serve!

One last word about spiritual gifts: there are many today who strongly emphasize what are generally considered "spectacular gifts." Paul warns against making one gift more important than another in the body of Christ:

If the foot shall say, because I am not the hand, I am not of the body; *is it therefore not of the body* (I Corinthians 12:15; read also I Corinthians 12:16-27)?

How I praise Thee, precious Savior,   **Channels Only**
That Thy love laid hold of me,   Mary E. Maxwell
Thou hast saved and cleansed
And filled me,
That I might Thy channel be!

XV

Fruit of the Spirit

(For the fruit of the Spirit is in all goodness and righteousness and truth:)
proving what is acceptable unto the Lord (Ephesians 5:9-10).

When God gives spiritual gifts to believers He gives them the power and ability to serve Him. Sometimes, however, Christians wonder if they have the proper *temperament* to be effective for the Lord. This is undoubtedly why God produces the fruit of the Spirit.

Fruit grows at a gradual pace; and so it is reasonable to expect the fruit of the Spirit to grow in a similar manner. This is not something Christians have to seek or pray for; it is an automatic aspect of their salvation.

Scripture has quite a bit to say about fruit in general. Below is a list that   should prove to be helpful:

1. **God is the source of virtue and fruit in lives.**
    Abide in Me, and I in you. As the branch cannot bear fruit of itself, except it abide in the vine: no more can ye, except ye abide in Me. *I am the vine, ye are the branches...* (John 15:4-5a).

2. **God gets good results when He plants His fruit.**
    He that abideth in Me, and I in him, *the same bringeth forth much fruit:* for without Me ye can do nothing (John 15:5b).

3. **God the Father receives the glory when fruit is produced.**
    Herein is My Father glorified, that ye bear much fruit: so shall ye be my disciples. As the Father hath loved Me, so have I loved you: continue ye in My love (John 15:8-9).

4. **In the end, God will destroy all that is unfruitful.**
    Bring forth therefore fruits meet for repentance: And think not to say within yourselves, We have Abraham to our father: for I say unto you, that God is able of these stones to raise up children unto Abraham. And now also the axe is laid to the root of the trees: *therefore every tree which bringeth not forth good fruit is hewn down, and cast into the fire* (Matthew 3:8-10).

5. **Fruit is a good indicator of the quality of spiritual life.**
    Ye shall know them by their fruits. Do men gather grapes of thorns, or figs of thistles? Even so every good tree bringeth forth good fruit; but a corrupt tree bringeth forth evil fruit. A good tree cannot bring forth evil fruit, neither can a corrupt tree bring forth good fruit. *Wherefore by their fruits ye shall know them* (Matthew 7:16-18, 20).

6. **Fruit is likened unto the resurrection and illustrates proper Christian living.**
And Jesus answered them, saying, The hour is come, that the Son of man should be glorified. Verily, verily, I say unto you, Except a corn of wheat fall into the ground and die, it abideth alone: *but if it die, it bringeth forth much fruit.* He that loveth his life shall lose it; and he that hateth his life in this world shall keep it unto life eternal (John 12:23-25).

7. **Lips can produce fruit of praise.**
By Him therefore *let us offer the sacrifice of praise continually, that is, the fruit of our lips,* giving thanks to His name (Hebrews 13:15).

8. **Growing fruit requires patience (because it is a process).**
But that on the good ground are they, which in an honest and good heart, having heard the Word, keep it, *and bring forth fruit with patience* (Luke 8:15).

9. **God intends that fruit be long lasting.**
Ye have not chosen Me, but I have chosen you, and ordained you, that ye should go and bring forth fruit, *and that your fruit should remain...* (John 15:16).

The Scriptures also have quite a bit to say about the fruit of the Spirit.

But the fruit of the Spirit is *love, joy, peace, longsuffering, gentleness, goodness, faith, Meekness, temperance:* against such there is no law (Galatians 5:22-23).

1. **The fruit of the Spirit is in great contrast to the works of the flesh.**
Now the works of the flesh are manifest, which are these: Adultery, fornication, uncleanness, lasciviousness, Idolatry, witchcraft, hatred, variance, emulations, wrath, strife, seditions, heresies, Envyings, murders, drunkenness, revellings, and such like: of the which I tell you before, as I have also told you in time past, that *they which do such things shall not inherit the kingdom of God* (Galatians 5:19-21).

2. **The Holy Spirit produces a special kind of love.**
This is the *agape* love which is mentioned often in Scripture.

But God commendeth His love toward us, in that, while we were yet sinners, Christ died for us (Romans 5:8).

This word *agape* has an amazing history in the Greek language. If you were to look up this word in a classical Greek lexicon, you would be amazed at how seldom the word is used and how little significance it really had until the Judeo-Christian community began to use it.

Greek has a history that pre-dates Homer. Philosophers, poets, mathematicians, architects, historians, and writers of plays wrote significant pieces of literature in their fields, but they simply did not understand the love that is revealed in God's Word; and when it came time for the translators of the Hebrew Old Testament to translate God's love into a Greek word, there really wasn't one that accurately conveyed the meaning! Their best choice was to take this word *agape,* which had little meaning, and give it significance it never had before.

The world simply does not understand this love until it sees it demonstrated in the lives of believers or the Holy Spirit moves in minds and hearts, revealing God's great love to them through His Word and Christ's redeeming death on the cross.

3. *The Holy Spirit produces joy.*
There is a significant difference between happiness and joy. Simply put, happiness is generally based on circumstances and is something that can change easily, based on outward circumstances.

On the other hand, *joy* is a settled condition which does not change easily. This is what the Holy Spirit offers.

To illustrate the difference, a believer may not be *happy* that a loved one is apparently on his/her deathbed, but he can have the *joy* that only comes from God that their family member/friend is saved and will soon be with the Lord. The joy of the Lord is much more satisfying than simple happiness!

God's Word does not change; so take joy in that! Salvation is a gift from God; so take joy in that! We can have close fellowship with our Lord; so take joy in that!

Every good gift and every perfect gift is from above, and cometh down from the Father of lights, with Whom is no variableness, neither shadow of turning (James 4:17).

4. *The Holy Spirit produces peace.*
The world has its idea of what peace is, but God produces something much better!

When a man's ways please the Lord, *He maketh his enemies to be at peace with him* (Proverbs 16:7).

Peace I leave with you; My peace I give unto you: *not as the world giveth, give I unto you.* Let not your heart be troubled, neither let it be afraid (John 14:27).

To many *peace* is simply a cessation of hostilities which may very well be resumed at any time. God's peace, however, is much deeper and eternal.

Therefore being justified by faith, *we have peace with God through our Lord Jesus Christ:* By Whom also we have access by faith into this grace wherein we stand, and rejoice in hope of the glory of God (Romans 5:1-2).

5. *The Holy Spirit produces longsuffering.*
The Greek noun here is *makrothumia.* It is a compound word, made up of *macros* (which means "long, distant") and *thumos* (which means "passion, hot anger, wrath"). The basic meaning of the word, then, is "not easily made angry."

Put on therefore, as the elect of God, holy and beloved, bowels of mercies, kindness, humbleness of mind, meekness, *longsuffering, Forbearing one another,* if any man have a quarrel against any: even as Christ forgave you, so also do ye. And above all these things put on charity, which is the bond of perfectness (Colossians 3:12-14).

There is no doubt that from time to time we face heartbreak and poor treatment in this world. Sometimes even friends disappoint us with their attitudes and actions. In fact, we are sometimes wronged. Ephesians 4:26-27 indicates what kind of reactions we should have when these things happen to us:

Be ye angry, and sin not: *let not the sun go down upon your wrath:* Neither give place to the devil.

It is one thing to be "righteously indignant" about sin. God hates sin, and so should we, but *remaining* angry is called sin in this passage. It is an unhealthy thing to go to bed at night angry with God or anybody else (this is the meaning of the words "let not the sun go down upon your wrath"). Satan can use anger in our lives to produce frustration and bitterness. This is why the Holy Spirit is also working in the lives of believers to produce longsuffering.

6. *The Holy Spirit produces gentleness.*
The basic idea of the Greek noun *chrestotes* is "kindness." Probably the most appropriate theological definition of kindness is "love in action."

When a person falls in love, he/she is always trying to find ways to express that love for the other person. These ways include compliments, gifts, all kinds of loving sentiments. Kindness finds a way to express love!

That is exactly what the Holy Spirit is doing for all believers. He is giving us the right attitude and an ability to express our love for others in this world. What an important ministry the Holy Spirit has when He does this in the lives of believers!

One hymn writer certainly expressed this idea well:

Faith of our Fathers!
We will love
Both friend and foe
In all our strife:
And preach Thee, too
As love knows how,
By kindly words
And virtuous life.

Faith of Our Fathers
Frederick W. Faber

To speak evil of no man, to be no brawlers, but gentle, showing all meekness unto all men. For we ourselves were sometimes foolish, disobedient, deceived, serving divers lusts and pleasures, living in malice and envy, hateful, and hating one another. *But after that the kindness and love of God our Savior toward man appeared* (Titus 3:2-4).

As we have therefore opportunity, *let us do good unto all men, especially unto them who are of the household of faith* (Galatians 6:10).

7. *The Holy Spirit produces goodness.*

The Greek noun here is *agathosune.* The basic idea of this word is "inward goodness." There is another word in Greek (*kalos* and related words) which generally means "outward goodness, beauty." Thus the goodness which the Holy Spirit produces is a goodness of character. He works in the lives of believers in such a way that their motives are pure.

It is possible to do good things and yet not always have a pure motive. That is why God works to produce *goodness* in the hearts and lives of Christians. This goodness surely involves sincerity.

Wherefore also we pray always for you, *that our God would count you worthy of this calling, and fulfill all the good pleasure of His goodness,* and the work of faith with power: That the name of our Lord Jesus Christ may be glorified in you, and ye in Him, according to the grace of our God and the Lord Jesus Christ (II Thessalonians 1:11-12).

I speak not by commandment, but by occasion of the forwardness of others, *and to prove the sincerity of your love.* Wherefore show ye to them, and before the churches, the proof of your love, and of our boasting on your behalf (II Corinthians 2:8, 24).

8. *The Holy Spirit produces faith.*

We will deal with the whole subject of faith later in the book, but suffice it to say here that many Christians can correctly testify to the fact that their faith in God and His Word has grown as they have gotten older. No doubt this is why so many of the "senior saints" have very significant prayer lives.

The Holy Spirit works in the lives of believers to increase and perfect faith.

Jesus saith unto him, If thou canst believe, all things are possible to him that believeth. And straightway the father of the child cried out, and said with tears, *Lord, I believe; help Thou mine unbelief* (Mark 9:23-24).

9. *The Holy Spirit produces meekness.*

"Meekness is not weakness," so the old saying goes. That is certainly true. It takes a lot of character and integrity to remain meek in this world. Probably the best simple definition of meekness is "proper self-evaluation."

On the one hand, if we were to look at ourselves, we would see sin, weakness, and misery. If that is *all* we see when we look at ourselves, we will surely fail in our service to God! But thanks be to God, that is only part of the picture!

He has forgiven us. He has given us positions which have dignity. He has made us holy and declared that fact in His court. He has given us spiritual gifts and is producing fruit in our lives. It is no wonder, then, that the Apostle Paul emphasizes Who is the source of success in his life:

I can do all things through Christ which strengtheneth me (Philippians 4:13).

Paul could not perform his ministry in his own strength, and neither can we, but he understood that with God's working in his life great things could and would be accomplished for His glory.

Listed below are some Biblical thoughts on meekness:

The meek *shall eat and be satisfied: they shall praise the Lord...* (Psalm 22:26a).

The meek *will He guide in judgment:* and the meek *will He teach His way* (Psalm 25:9).

But the meek *shall inherit the earth;* and shall *delight themselves in the abundance of peace* (Psalm 37:11).

Take my yoke upon you, and learn of Me; for I am meek and lowly in heart: and *ye shall find rest unto your souls* (Matthew 11:29).

10. *The Holy Spirit produces temperance.*

The Greek noun here means "mastery, self-control." There are those who feel the Holy Spirit causes people to be just a bit out of control or in some sort of mania, but the self-control the Holy Spirit produces is very different from that. If anything, the Holy Spirit produces order in the life of a believer.

Here is some of what the Scriptures teach about temperance:

A. Self-control is vital to serving God.
   Know ye not that they which run in a race run all, but one receiveth the prize? So run, that ye may obtain. And every man that striveth for the mastery *is temperate in all things.* Now they do it to obtain a corruptible crown; but we an incorruptible. I therefore so run, not as uncertainly; so fight I, not as one that beateth the air. *But I keep under my body, and bring it into subjection: Lest that by any means, when I have preached to others, I myself should be a castaway* (I Corinthians 9:24-27).

B. Moderation is important in our testimony before God and men.
   Let your moderation be known unto all men. The Lord is at hand (Philippians 4:5).

C. We should moderate in how we eat food.
   Hast thou found honey? *Eat so much as is sufficient for thee,* lest thou be filled therewith, and vomit it (Proverbs 25:16).

D. Churches are to teach moderation to its older men.
   But speak thou the things which become sound doctrine: *That the aged men be sober, grave, temperate, sound in faith, in charity, in patience* (Titus 2:1-2).

Joys are flowing like a river
Since the Comforter has come;
He abides with us forever,
Makes the trusting heart His home.

Blessed Quietness
Manie P. Ferguson

Blessed quietness, holy quietness,
What assurance in my soul!
On the stormy sea, He speaks peace to me,
How the billows cease to roll!

What a wonderful salvation,
Where we always see His face!
What a perfect habitation,
What a quiet resting place!

XVI

Propitiation

My little children, these things write I unto you, that ye sin not. And if any man sin, we have an advocate with the Father, Jesus Christ the righteous: And He is the propitiation for our sins...(I John 2:1-2a).

Probably the most influential sermon ever preached in the English language was delivered by an old Puritan named Jonathan Edwards. That message was entitled "Sinners in the Hands of an Angry God."

In that sermon Edwards paints an awful picture. His listeners can see themselves as spiders hanging on a single thread of a web. Underneath is a huge raging fire! The only thing that is keeping the spider (you) from falling into that fire is God's grace, but if you do not repent, time will very quickly run out and you will suffer eternal loss as a result! What a situation! And yet it accurately describes unsaved man's dilemma.

This message was so powerful that a great revival spread throughout New England and students still read its words today. The reason it was so effective was that it emphasized an important Biblical truth: *God hates sin!*

The Scriptures are abundantly clear. Sin is serious and will be punished one way or the other.

Of course, for the Christian, Jesus paid that price!

One of the great results of His redemptive work on the cross is *the removal of the Father's anger against sinners.* This is the classic definition of "propitiation."

Some confuse propitiation with expiation, but there is an important difference. The word "expiation" means "a gaining of favor," whereas "propitiation" involves the removal of wrath.

The Scriptures give a clear indication that God does get angry with sin:

1. ***A lack of faith in Christ brings eternal punishment.***
   He that believeth on the Son hath everlasting life: and *he that believeth not the Son shall not see life; but the wrath of God abideth on him* (John 3:36).

   And I saw a great white throne, and Him that sat on it, from Whose face the earth and the heaven fled away; and there was found no place for them. And I saw the dead, small and great, stand before God; and the books were opened: and another book was opened, which is the book of life: and the dead were judged out of those things which were written, according to their works. And the sea gave up the dead which were in it: and death and hell delivered up the dead which were in them: and they were judged every man according to their works. And death and hell were cast into the lake of fire. This is the second death. *And whosoever was not found written in the book of life was cast into the lake of fire* (Revelation 20:11-15).

2. **Ungodliness in this world causes God to be angry.**
For the wrath of God is revealed from heaven against all ungodliness and unrighteousness of men, who hold the truth in unrighteousness (Romans 1:18).

3. **God's punishment extended even to the Jewish people in the wilderness.**
Wherefore (as the Holy Ghost saith, Today if ye will hear His voice, Harden not your hearts, as in the provocation, in the day of temptation in the wilderness: *When your fathers tempted Me, and saw my works forty years. Wherefore I was grieved with that generation,* and said, They do always err in their heart, and they have not known My ways. *So I swore in my wrath, They shall not enter into My rest.*). Take heed, brethren, lest there be in any of you an evil heart of unbelief, in departing from the living God (Hebrews 3:7-12).

4. **God's wrath will be poured out fearfully during the tribulation.**
And the heaven departed as a scroll when it is rolled together; and every mountain and island were moved out of their places. And the kings of the earth, and the great men, and the rich men, and the chief captains, and the mighty men, and every bondman, and every free man, hid themselves in the dens and in the rocks of the mountains; And said to the mountains and rocks, Fall on us, and hide us from the face of Him that sitteth on the throne, and from the wrath of the Lamb: *For the great day of His wrath is come; and who shall be able to stand* (Revelation 6:14-17)?

Four main points can be made about propitiation:

1. **Jesus is the Provider of our propitiation.**
...we have an advocate with the Father, Jesus Christ the righteous: *And He is the propitiation for our sins: and not for ours only, but also for the sins of the whole world* (I John 2:1b-2).

2. **Jesus' blood was the price of our propitiation.**
Being justified freely by His grace through the redemption that is in Christ Jesus: *Whom God hath set forth to be a propitiation through faith in His blood,* to declare His righteousness for the remission of sins that are past, through the forbearance of God: To declare, I say, at this time His righteousness: that He might be just, and the justifier of him which believeth in Jesus (Romans 3:24-26).

3. **The Father's wrath was appeased by the work of Christ on our behalf.**

Wherefore in all things it behooved Him to be made like unto His brethren, that He might be a merciful and faithful high priest in things pertaining to God, *to make reconciliation for the sins of the people* (Hebrews 2:17).

4. *Propitiation is a great demonstration of the Father's love toward His own.*
In this was manifested the love of God toward us, because that God sent His only begotten Son into the world, that we might live through Him. Herein is love, not that we loved God, *but that He loved us, and sent His Son to be the propitiation for our sins.* Beloved, if God so loved us, we ought also to love one another (I John 4:9-11).

One more important point here: repentance is also important in bringing about propitiation. It is God Who works in us to bring about repentance:

And thinkest thou this, O man, that judgest them which do such things, and doest the same, That thou shalt escape the judgment of God? Or despisest thou the riches of His goodness and forbearance and longsuffering; not knowing that *the goodness of God leadeth thee to repentance* (Romans 2:3-4)?

Dark is the stain **Grace Greater than**
That we cannot hide, **Our Sin**
What can avail to take it away? Julia H.
Look! There is flowing a crimson tide; Johnston
Whiter than snow you may be today!

Grace, grace, God's grace;
Grace that will pardon and cleanse within;
Grace, grace, God's grace,
Grace that is greater than all our sin!

XVII

Reconciliation

We pray you in Christ's stead, Be ye reconciled to God. For He hath made Him to be sin for us, Who knew no sin, that we might be made the righteousness of God in Him (II Corinthians 5:20b-21).

The Greek verbs *allasso* and *katallasso* are the main words under consideration when it comes to reconciliation. The adjective *allos* means "other" and is at the heart of the meaning of both words. *Allasso* usually means "to change, to transform;" *katallasso* is similar in meaning: "to change, to make other than it is."

When these words are used in a context that involves a bad relationship between people, the change that takes place for the better is translated "reconciliation."

Propitiation is the removal of God's wrath; reconciliation is the restoration to fellowship between God and those who are saved.

There are many indications that before salvation the relationship between God and man is not good. In fact, the Scriptures say that we were His enemies. Listed below are some verses which demonstrate this point:

Ye adulterers and adulteresses, know ye not that *the friendship of the world is enmity With God?* Whosoever therefore will be a friend of the world is the enemy of God (James 4:4).

No man can serve two masters: for *either he will hate the one, and love the other; or else he will hold to the one, and despise the other.* Ye cannot serve God and mammon (Matthew 6:24).

As concerning the Gospel, *they are enemies for your sakes...* (Romans 11:28a).

And having made peace through the blood of His cross, by Him to reconcile all things unto Himself; by Him, I say, whether they be things in earth, or things in heaven. *And you, that were sometimes alienated and enemies in your mind* by wicked works yet now hath He reconciled (Colossians 1:20-21).

(For many walk, of whom I have told you often, and now tell you even weeping, that *they are the enemies of the cross of Christ:* Whose end is destruction, whose God is their belly, and whose glory is in their shame, who mind earthly things)—Philippians 3:18-19.

In reconciliation, however, bad situations are made much better. Paul speaks of this potentiality in a marriage relationship:

And unto the married, I command, yet not I, but the Lord, Let not the wife depart from her husband: But and if she depart, let her remain unmarried, *or be reconciled to her husband:* and let not the husband put away his wife (I Corinthians 7:10-11).

Concerning the *changes* that take place,

1. Believers have new life.
    Marvel not, my brethren, if the world hate you. *We know we have passed from death unto life, because we love the brethren.* He that loveth not his brother abideth in death (I John 3:13-14).

2. Believers, once God's enemies, are now His friends.
    And the Scripture was fulfilled which saith, Abraham believed God, and it was imputed unto him for righteousness: *and he was called the Friend of God* (James 2:23).

3. God goes so far as to call believers His brothers.
    But we see Jesus, Who was made a little lower than the angels for the suffering of the death, crowned with glory and honor; that He by the grace of God should taste death for every man. For it became Him, for Whom are all things, and by Whom are all things, in bringing many sons to glory, to make the Captain of their salvation perfect through sufferings. For both He that sanctifieth and they who are sanctified are all of one: for which cause *He is not ashamed to call them brethren* (Hebrews 2:9-11).

    Interestingly enough, we have a clear indication of how this brother/brother relationship is:

    ...and there is *a friend that sticketh closer than a brother* (Proverbs 18:24b).

To conclude these thoughts, a believer has been brought into God's family by Spirit baptism, has been adopted into God's family as a fully adult son with many privileges, has been propitiated from God's wrath, and has a friendship and brotherly relationship with God!

Surely God longs to have fellowship with His own! He has provided everything possible to make a good relationship possible! The only question is whether or not we will allow Him that closeness. Below is a great verse which indicates the relationship which is possible.

Behold, I stand at the door, and knock: if any man hear My voice, and open the door, *I will come in to him, and will sup with him, and he with Me* (Revelation 3:20).

There is a place of quiet rest,
Near to the heart of God,
A place where sin cannot molest
Near to the heart of God.

There is a place of full release
Near to the heart of God,
A place where all is joy and peace,
Near to the heart of God.

O Jesus, blest Redeemer,
Sent from the heart of God,
Hold us who wait before Thee,
Near to the heart of God!

Near to the Heart
Of God
Cleland B. McAfee

XVIII

Forgiveness

Purge me with hyssop, and I shall be clean: wash me, and I shall be whiter than snow (Psalm 51:7).

There are many today who do not *feel* forgiven even though they have sincerely asked God (and anybody else who was wronged) for forgiveness. In some of these cases the misery of feeling unforgiven lasts for decades.

If sin remains unconfessed, of course, God cannot forgive.

On the other hand, it is important for all to understand what the Scriptures teach about this crucial subject.

Feelings change, especially as conditions in our lives seem to be constantly changing. What kind of reactions do we have when a boss at work seems to be very reasonable one minute and quite rude a minute later? Obviously, such instability can create considerable chaos in a workplace.

We must realize that God's nature *does not change.* When He makes a promise He will keep it because He is holy and cannot lie.

Here are three Biblical truths in this regard:

1. **God is eternal.**
   Before the mountains were brought forth, or ever Thou hadst formed the earth and the world, *even from everlasting to everlasting Thou art God* (Psalm 90:2).

2. **God is immutable (does not change).**
   Jesus Christ *the same yesterday, today, and for ever* (Hebrews 13:8).

3. **God is holy.**
   Therefore hearken unto me, ye men of understanding: *be it far from God, that He should do this wickedness*...that He should commit iniquity (Job 34:10).

   I have not spoken in secret, in a dark place of the earth: I said not unto the seed of Jacob, Seek ye Me in vain: *I the Lord speak righteousness, I declare things that are right* (Isaiah 45:19).

These things being so, we can be sure that God means what He says and says what He means. We can also be sure that He will not change His mind after making a promise.

The Bible has quite a bit to say about forgiveness in general:

1. A heart that is right with God does not want to "get even," even when it has been wronged.
   Say not, I will do so to him as he hath done to me: I will render to the man according to his work (Proverbs 24:29).

2. It is not a good thing to stay angry, but rather to forgive.
   The discretion of a man deferreth his anger; and it is his glory to pass over a transgression (Proverbs 19:11).

3. We should both forgive and pray for those who owe us something.
   And forgive us our debts, as we forgive our debtors (Matthew 6:12).

4. An unwillingness to forgive others causes God not to forgive us.
   But if ye forgive not men their trespasses, neither will your Father forgive your trespasses (Matthew 6:15).

5. We should forgive as often as necessary.
   Then came Peter to Him, and said, Lord, how oft shall my brother sin against me, and I forgive Him? Till seven times? Jesus saith unto him, I say not unto thee, *Until seven times: but, Until seventy times seven* (Matthew 18:21-22).

6. Forgiveness should be conditioned on repentance from the offender.
   Take heed to yourselves: if thy brother trespass against thee, rebuke him; *and if he repent, forgive him* (Luke 17:3).

7. We should always be ready to forgive.
   And be ye kind one to another, tenderhearted, *forgiving one another, even as God for Christ's sake hath forgiven you* (Ephesians 4:32).

Here is a list of references that completely explains God's forgiveness in the life of a believer:

1. When God forgives sin, He removes and forgets it!
   As far as the east is from the west, so far hath He removed our transgressions from us (Psalm 103:12).

   And their sins and iniquities will I remember no more. Now where remission of these is, there is no more offering for sin (Hebrews 10:17-18).

2. God's forgiveness involves a total cleansing which is based on confession.
   Iniquities prevail against me: as for our transgressions, *Thou shalt purge them away* (Psalm 65:3).

   If we confess our sins, He is faithful and just to forgive us our sins, *and to cleanse us from all unrighteousness* (I John 1:9).

3. God forgives all sin.
    Thou hast forgiven the iniquity of Thy people, *Thou hast covered all their sin.* Selah (Psalm 85:2).

4. Confession of sin creates a wonderful relationship between the believer, God, and fellow believers.

    That which we have seen and heard declare we unto you, that ye may have fellowship with us: and truly our fellowship is with the Father, and with His Son Jesus Christ. And these things write we unto you, that your joy may be full. This then is the message which we have heard of Him, and declare unto you, that God is light, and in Him is no darkness at all. If we say that we have fellowship with Him, and walk in darkness, we lie, and do not the truth: *But if we walk in the light as He is in the light, we have fellowship one with another, and the blood of Jesus Christ His Son cleanseth us from all sin* (I John 1:3-7).

5. Christ's blood makes God's forgiveness possible.
    Being justified freely by His grace through the redemption that is in Christ Jesus: *Whom God hath set forth to be a propitiation through faith in His blood,* to declare His righteousness for the remission of sins that are past, through the forbearance of God (Romans 3:24-25).

A few words should be said about the words "repentance" and "confession." Both these words are important because they have a lot to do with God's forgiveness in our lives.

The noun for repentance is *metanoia* in the Greek. This word literally means "a change of mind." Repentance involves an emotional element (sorrow), an intellectual element (acknowledgement), and a volitional element (a determination of the will never to go back to sin). This word is used primarily to describe what must happen when a sinner comes to God for salvation.

The verb "to confess" is *homologeo* in the Greek. This word literally means "to say the same thing, to take the same attitude." Confession also has the emotional, intellectual, and volitional elements to it. This word is used primarily to describe what must happen when a believer stumbles into sin and needs to restore fellowship with God.

In repentance, a person totally changes his mind, his attitude, and his determination to do what is right. He recognizes that it is God Who can forgive and help him to live completely for Him.

In confession, a person approaches God and asks Him to make him react the same way about sin that He does. Obviously, God hates sin; so when a believer genuinely confesses his sin, he is asking God to help him to hate sin and avoid it. This is God's way of providing an opportunity to have great fellowship with Him.

In conclusion, when sin is dealt with as God directs, He really forgives! It really is not a matter of how one might *feel about it*. In reality, it is a matter of God's faithfulness. He has promised to do so if we genuinely approach Him with the right attitude.

Arise, My Soul, Arise
Charles Wesley

Arise, my soul arise,
Shake off thy guilty fears;
The Savior's sacrifice
In my behalf appears;
Before the throne my surety stands.
Before the throne my surety stands:
My name is written on His hands!

Now I am reconciled;
God's pardoning voice I hear;
He owns me for His child;
I can no longer fear;
With confidence I now draw nigh,
With confidence I now draw nigh:
And, "Father, Abba, Father," cry!

XIX

Sealing

Now He which stablisheth us with you in Christ, and hath anointed us, is God;
Who hath sealed us, and given the earnest of the Spirit in our hearts
(II Corinthians 1:21-22).

When a child is born a birth certificate is issued. When a piece of property or an automobile is paid for a title is issued. When one successfully completes a college degree program a diploma is granted.

In most cases a "seal" is easily seen on all these documents.

According to the Scriptures, when God saves a soul He places a seal on that important transaction.

The idea of having seals and official state insignias is an old one. For instance, when our Lord died and was buried, there were those who were concerned that the disciples might try to steal His body from the grave and then claim that He rose from the dead. When Pilate heard about this he determined to place the seal of the Roman government at the burial site:

Pilate said unto them, Ye have a watch: go your way, make it as sure as ye can. So they went, and made the sepulcher sure, *sealing the stone,* and setting a watch (Matthew 27:65-66).

There are three passages in the New Testament which give us this precious doctrine of sealing:

1. *II Corinthians 1:21-22.*
Now He which stablisheth us with you in Christ, and hath anointed us, is God; *Who hath sealed us,* and given the earnest of the Holy Spirit in our hearts.

Four important points can be made from these verses:

God the Father establishes the believer in Christ.

God the Father anoints the believer.

God the Father seals the believer.

God the Father gives the Holy Spirit as an earnest (a downpayment) to the believer. The promise is that eternal life and better conditions await the believer in heaven.

2. ***Ephesians 1:13-14.***
   In Whom ye also trusted, after that ye heard the Word of truth, the Gospel of your salvation: in Whom also after that ye believed, *ye were sealed with that Holy Spirit of promise,* Which is the earnest of our inheritance until the redemption of the purchased possession, unto the praise of His glory.

   Two important points can be made from these verses:

   The sealing took place after belief in Christ.

   Believers are sealed with the Holy Spirit.

3. ***Ephesians 4:30.***
   And grieve not the Holy Spirit of God, *whereby ye were sealed unto the day of redemption.*

   Two important points can be made from this verse:

   The word translated "ye are sealed" is in the aorist tense in the Greek, indicating a completed action. Believers are immediately sealed the moment they are saved.

   The sealing lasts until "the day of redemption." This means that until the Lord calls the believer to heaven the sealing of the Holy Spirit is upon his soul.

There is a logical connection between sanctification, justification, and sealing. In positional sanctification the believer is *made* holy in his standing before God. In justification he is *declared* holy by God. In sealing, the record is *made official* in the court of heaven.

Satan can make whatever accusation he wants against a believer. It simply doesn't matter. Why? A believer has been sanctified, justified, and sealed, and God did it all!

Generally speaking, sealing involves such things as security, official status, ownership, and a guarantee. These things are granted to all believers. They are precious truths that the Bible teaches clearly, and they cannot be taken away or nullified.

We praise Thee for Thy Spirit, Lord,
The Blessed Holy Ghost,
The promised Comforter from heav'n
Who came at Pentecost.

We praise Thee for His sovereign grace
That broke our darkness through,
And wrought within us by Thy Word
A birth Divinely new.

We praise Thee that He is the seal
Whereby we're marked as Thine
Until redemption's day shall dawn
And we in glory shine!

**We Praise Thee
For Thy Spirit,
Lord**
Harold P. Barker

XX

Liberty

If the Son therefore shall make you free, ye shall be free indeed
(John 8:36).

When Jesus spoke the words of John 8:36 (quoted above), ¾ of the world was in slavery. The only way for parents to get themselves and their children out of slavery was to pay a great price. In the vast majority of cases people never did get out of slavery during their life on this earth.

Today soldiers labor and sometimes die in an attempt to provide security and liberty to the citizens of their country. The efforts that they make are at best temporary, because there are always outside forces working to enslave or dominate, and soldiers of the next generation will be called upon to continue the process.

In salvation, however, God offers a freedom that is eternal.

The Bible has quite a bit to say about the freedom God provides. Listed below are some of the great revealed truths about it:

1. **The truth is the way to freedom.**
    Then said Jesus to those Jews which believed on Him, If ye continue in My Word, then are ye My disciples indeed; *And ye shall know the truth, and the truth shall make you free* (John 8:31-32).

    Truth ultimately is found in Jesus Christ (John 14:6) and God's Word (John 17:17). There are many sources that offer information, some of it true, but in the end it is God Who is the only One Who knows all things and cannot lie.

    There are many *wrong* answers to the simple arithmetic of "2 plus 2 equals what?" There is only one *correct* answer. Truth is actually a very narrow thing!

    When it comes to spiritual matters, religion offers many ideas about salvation, but God offers only one way. That one way is through Jesus Christ (Acts 4:12). Religion offers bondage to rules, regulations, teachings, traditions. Our Savior offers eternal life.

2. **God offers freedom of choice in many matters as long as it is not sinful.**
    Conscience, I say, not thine own, but of the other: *for why is my liberty judged of another man's conscience?* For if I by grace be a partaker, why am I evil spoken of for that for which I give thanks? Whether therefore ye eat, or drink, or whatsoever ye do, do all to the glory of God. Give none offense, neither to the Jews, nor to the Gentiles, nor to the church of God (I Corinthians 10:29-32).

Him that is weak in the faith receive ye, but not to doubtful disputations. For one believeth that he may eat all things: another, who is weak, eateth herbs. Let not him that eateth despise him that eateth not; and let not him which eateth not judge him that eateth: for God hath received him (Romans 14:1-2; read also Romans 14:5-8).

These two passages speak of freedom of conscience in Christianity when it pertains to certain foods. Some feel it is good to eat foods that others feel is wrong. God is saying that as long as there is no direct prohibition against a certain food, then it is a matter of conscience. The believer can make up his own mind about what to do or not do in these cases.

The Bible is not a "rules manual" that tells us the right and wrong of *every* issue we may face. It is, rather, a book that spells out what is right or wrong in certain areas, allowing liberty in other areas.

There are two main considerations that should be understood about this liberty. In all matters we are to "do all to the glory of God" (I Corinthians 10:31). God wants us to have hearts that seek to honor Him. The second matter is the conscience of those who may disagree with our own conclusions. We are entitled to our convictions, but we are obligated not to offend a brother for whom Christ died.

In other words, if we feel something is perfectly acceptable to God and we are seeking to honor Him in the matter, when we come into contact with a brother who feels it is wrong (and he is also seeking to honor God), then we should abstain from that thing. Why? The principle is that we would then be offending a brother when it is totally unnecessary and unwise to do so. We are, however, entitled to our own feelings and convictions about these kinds of things. God provides liberty for us in these matters.

3. *The presence of the Holy Spirit produces liberty.*
Now the Lord is that Spirit: *and where the Spirit of the Lord is, there is liberty* (II Corinthians 3:17).

4. *There are many who would like to destroy the liberty that Christ offers.*
And that because of false brethren unawares brought in, who came privily to spy out our liberty which we have in Christ Jesus, *that they might bring us into bondage* (Galatians 2:4).

There were false teachers in Galatia during Paul's day who were known as "Judaizers." These men tried to add such things as circumcision and certain Jewish traditions as requirements for salvation. Paul would have NONE of that, and neither should we! Salvation is by grace through faith plus *nothing.* To see Paul's reaction to these false teachers, read Galatians 1:6-9.

5. ***Believers need to stand up against the false teaching that destroys liberty.***
Stand fast therefore in the liberty wherewith Christ hath made us free, *and be not entangled again with the yoke of bondage.* Behold, I Paul say unto you, that if ye be circumcised, Christ shall profit you nothing (Galatians 5:1-2).

In verse 2 Paul is pointing out the error of depending on circumcision for salvation. The Gospel is not to be perverted. Adding to it or taking away from it is a very serious matter!

6. ***Christian liberty should never be used as an excuse to sin.***
For so is the will of God, that with well doing ye may put to silence the ignorance of foolish men: As free, *and not using your liberty for a cloak of maliciousness,* but as servants of God (I Peter 2:15-16).

What shall we say then? *Shall we continue in sin, that grace may abound? God forbid.* How shall we, that are dead to sin, live any longer therein (Romans 6:1-2)?

For, brethren, ye have been called unto liberty, only *use not liberty for an occasion to the flesh,* but by love serve one another (Galatians 5:13).

7. ***God's liberty produces good results.***
For if any be a hearer of the Word, and not a doer, he is like a man beholding his face in a glass: For he beholdeth himself, and goeth his way, and straightway for-getteth what manner of man he was. But *whoso looketh into the perfect law of liberty, and continueth therein, he being not a forgetful hearer, but a doer of the work, this man shall be blessed in his deed* (James 1:23-25).

8. ***God's liberty judges wrongdoing.***
For whosoever shall keep the whole law, and yet offend in one point, he is guilty of all. For he that said, Do not commit adultery, also said, Do not kill. Now if thou commit no adultery, yet if thou kill, thou art a transgressor of the law. So speak ye, and so do, *as they that shall be judged by the law of liberty* (James 2:10-12).

9. ***God's liberty brings great deliverance!***
Because the creature itself shall be delivered from the bondage of corruption into the glorious liberty of the children of God (Romans 8:21).

10. ***Freedom in Christ allows believers to serve God.***
Being then made free from sin, ye became the servants of righteousness. I speak after the manner of men because of the infirmity of your flesh: for ye have yielded your members servants to uncleanness and to iniquity unto iniquity; even so now yield your members servants to righteousness unto holiness. For when ye were the servants of sin, ye were free from righteousness. What fruit had ye then

in those things whereof ye are now ashamed? For the end of those things is death. *But now being made free from sin, and become servants of God, ye have your fruit unto holiness, and the end everlasting life* (Romans 6:18-22).

At Calvary
William R.
Newell

Years I spent in vanity and pride,
Caring not my Lord was crucified,
Knowing not it was for me He died
On Calvary!

Oh, the love that drew salvation's plan!
Oh, the grace that brought it down to Man!
Oh, the mighty gulf that God did span,
On Calvary!

Mercy there was great
And grace was free!
Pardon there was multiplied to me;
There my burdened soul found liberty,
At Calvary!

XXI

Success in Spiritual Warfare

Wherefore take unto you the whole armor of God, that ye may be able to withstand in the evil day; and having done all, to stand
(Ephesians 6:13).

Warfare has been a reality throughout human history. Study the ancient Babylonians, Assyrians, Greeks, Egyptians, or Romans and it becomes clear that either winning or losing in military campaigns dominates any serious discussion about each civilization.

In those cases they were fighting other countries with their military might and genius. All those battles involved loss of life and great expense.

In the Christian life a battle of a different kind takes place regularly. The believer who is obedient to God will soon find that he will have success in his spiritual warfare.

First, we will look at what the Bible has to say about spiritual warfare in general:
1. ***It is a reality in this life.***
   This charge I commit unto thee, son Timothy, according to the prophecies which went before on thee, *that thou mayest war a good warfare:* Holding faith, and a good conscience: which some having put away concerning faith have made shipwreck (I Timothy 1:18-19).

2. ***Believers should expect a tough fight.***
   Thou therefore *endure hardness as a good soldier of Jesus Christ* (II Timothy 2:3).

3. ***Christ is our leader into battle.***
   For it became Him, for Whom are all things, and by Whom are all things, in bringing many sons into glory, *to make the Captain of their salvation perfect through sufferings* (Hebrews 2:10).

4. ***Much of the battle involves the mind of the believer in a battle against the flesh.***
   But I see another law in my members, warring against the law of my mind, and bringing me into captivity to the law of sin which is in my members. O wretched man that I am! Who shall deliver me from the body of this death? I thank God through Jesus Christ our Lord, *So then with the mind I myself serve the law of God; but with the flesh the law of sin* (Romans 7:23-25).

5. ***God's plan is to have us win in the battles of the mind.***
   (For the weapons of our warfare are not carnal, but mighty through God to the pulling down of strongholds:) *Casting down imaginations, and every high thing*

that exalteth itself against the knowledge of God, and bringing into captivity every thought to the obedience of Christ. And having in a readiness to revenge all disobedience , when your obedience is fulfilled (II Corinthians 10:4-6).

6. ***Various kinds of lusts are a major factor.***
From whence come wars and fightings among you? *Come they not hence, even of lusts that war in your members?* Ye lust, and have not: ye kill, and desire to have, and cannot obtain; ye fight and war, yet ye have not, because ye ask not. Ye adulterers and adulteresses, know ye not that the friendship of the world is enmity with God? Whosoever therefore will be a friend of the world is the enemy of God (James 4:1-2, 4).

7. ***Ultimately, the battle is against Satan and spiritual wickedness in high places.***
For we wrestle not against flesh and blood, but against principalities, against powers, against the rulers of the darkness of this world, *against spiritual wickedness in high places* (Ephesians 6:12).

Submit yourselves therefore to God. *Resist the devil,* and he will flee from you (James 4:7).

8. ***God provides all the armor believers need to win in battle.***
Wherefore take unto you the whole armor of God, that ye may be able to withstand in the evil day, and having done all, to stand. Stand therefore, having your loins girt about with truth, and having on the breastplate of righteousness: And your feet shod with the preparation of the Gospel of peace; Above all, taking the shield of faith, wherewith ye shall be able to quench all the fiery darts of the wicked. And take the helmet of salvation, and the sword of the Spirit, which is the Word of God: Praying always with all prayer and supplication in the Spirit, and watching thereunto with all perseverance and supplication for all saints (Ephesians 6:13-18).

We will not attempt to preach again all the excellent sermons which have already been delivered from this passage of Scripture, but a few simple observations might prove helpful.

Notice that every part of the soldier's body is protected except his back. A believer needs to have his full armor on and fight directly, not run!

The armor provides a wide variety of important spiritual blessings: truth, righteousness, the Gospel, faith, the Word of God, and the privilege of prayer. Surely God provides us what is needed!

Many good things happen during spiritual warfare. Believers will stand after the battle is over, having defeated the foe. In addition, he will have presented the Gospel to those who desperately need to hear its glorious message; he will have the confidence that Satan's "fiery darts" cannot harm him; and he will have the joy of praying for others who are fighting the same enemy.

It is interesting to note that the Word of God is actually the only truly offensive weapon listed. Actually, the Bible is the "sword of the Spirit" here, and it is to be used in both offense *and* defense. Because the Bible is so crucial in the spiritual battles we face, we do well to memorize it, hide it in our hearts, apply it, and thank God for it every day!

One little personal note here: the entire reason for writing this book is that Christians understand *Biblically* what happens when they are saved. The opinions of the author are irrelevant. God has revealed great truths which can help us win the battles that lie ahead, but we need to be familiar with what He has provided!

Next we will look at what God promises to those who overcome in spiritual battle:

He that hath an ear, let him hear what the Spirit saith unto the churches: *To him that overcometh will I give to eat of the hidden manna, and will give him a white stone,* and in the stone a new name written, which no man knoweth, saving he that receiveth it (Revelation 2:17).

And he that overcometh, and keepeth my works unto the end, *to him will I give power over the nations* (Revelation 2:26).

He that overcometh, *the same shall be clothed in white raiment...*(Revelation 3:5).

Him that overcometh will I make a pillar in the temple of My God, and he shall go no more out; and I will write upon him the name of My God; and the name of the city of My God, which is new Jerusalem, which cometh down out of heaven from My God: and I will write upon him My new name (Revelation 3:12).

To him that overcometh will I grant to sit with Me in My throne, even as I also overcame, and am set down with My Father in His throne (Revelation 3:21).

9. *He has overcome the world.*
These things I have spoken unto you, that in Me ye might have peace. In the world ye shall have tribulation: *but be of good cheer; I have overcome the world* (John 16:33).

10. *He has overcome death.*
Then cometh the end, when He shall have delivered up the kingdom to God, even the Father; when He shall have put down all rule and all authority and power.

For He must reign, till He hath put all enemies under His feet. *The last enemy that shall be destroyed is death* (I Corinthians 15:24-26).

Soldiers of Christ, arise,
And put your armor on,
Strong in the strength
Which God supplies
Through His eternal Son;
Strong in the Lord of hosts,
And in His mighty power,
Who in the strength of Jesus trusts
Is more than conqueror!

Soldiers of Christ, Arise
Charles Wesley

Section III: The Permanence of Our Salvation
Overview

For God so loved the world, that He gave His only begotten Son, that whosoever believeth in Him should not perish, but have everlasting life
(John 3:16).

Undoubtedly the most loved and most often quoted verse in all the Word of God is John 3:16 (quoted above). Children memorize it early and many songs have been written based on it.

This verse contains eleven ultimate truths. Nicodemus asked Jesus questions, and He had answers that covered everything from the Father's planning of salvation, to the importance of believing in Christ alone, to the possession of eternal life.

Below is an outline and brief notes on this great verse:

For God *The ultimate Potentate*
Whenever "God" is mentioned in Scripture, the reference is normally to God the Father unless there is something in the context that tells us about the Holy Spirit or Jesus. It is obvious that it was the Father Who sent His Son here.

God is the Creator and sustainer of all things. He is eternal, holy, and omniscient. Because He has done all this and has these amazing attributes, He is also the sovereign Ruler of all things. This is why He is listed here as the "ultimate Potentate."

so *The ultimate plan*
The word "so" does not mean "so much," but rather "in this way," and that suggests a plan from God the Father. In some existence known only to God, long before He created the heavens and the earth, He came up with the plan of salvation. No doubt Jesus and the Holy Spirit agreed, and the plan was made sure.

Jesus was to be virgin born, live a sinless life, bear the sins of the whole world in His body, shed His blood to pay for man's sin, be buried and in the grave for three days, and be raised from the dead to make the offer of eternal life legitimate.

loved *The ultimate passion*
This is the *agape* love that was discussed earlier in the chapter concerning the fruit of Spirit. How could a holy God allow His own Son to die for sinners such as we all are? The only possible answer is His amazing love!

the world *The ultimate population*
The blood of Christ is sufficient for all mankind, no matter how old, no matter whether they lived in ancient, medieval, or even modern times, no matter what an individual's situation might be. God loves the entire world, and Christ died for all in

it. It certainly breaks the great heart of God when people reject His Son and the message of the Gospel.

that He gave *The ultimate present*
What more valuable gift could God give in this plan than His Son, our Savior? He gave His Son with Whom He had close fellowship from all eternity, knowing that when He would bear our sins on the cross the fellowship would have to be broken for a period of time. What love!

Any parent reading this book realizes that seeing your child suffer is much more agonizing than going through the pain. God the Father endured that as well, willingly giving His *only Son*!

His only begotten Son *The ultimate Person*
The word translated "only begotten" is *monogenes* in the Greek and should be understood to indicate His special relationship with the Father and ability to save mankind.

He created all things, as did the Father (John 1:1-3), He is the Son of God (John 3:16), and the idea of His being begotten of the Father is expressed earlier this Gospel:

No man hath seen God at any time; the only begotten (*monogenes,* as in John 3:16) Son, *which is in the bosom of the Father,* He hath declared Him (John 1:18).

Jesus is both God (having been begotten of the Father) and man (having been born as a human from the womb of Mary).

The point, however, is that Jesus Christ is the only One Who could save mankind. He is God, and therefore sinless; He is man, and therefore capable of dying for man.

No other person who has ever lived (or ever will live, for that matter) meets those requirements.

that whosoever *The ultimate potential*
It really doesn't matter to God how rich, poor, educated, ignorant, or famous a person might be. God invites people from all backgrounds to the wonderful salvation He offers through His Son Jesus Christ.

And the Spirit and the bride say, Come. And let him that heareth say, Come. And let him that is athirst come. *And whosoever will, let him take of the water of life freely* (Revelation 22:17).

believeth in Him *The ultimate placement*
Some people have the idea that it takes a tremendous amount of faith in order to be saved. Frankly, it is *far more important* that whatever faith a person has be placed in the right Person (our Savior, Jesus Christ) than how much faith he might have.

And Jesus said unto them, Because of your unbelief: for verily I say unto you, *If ye have faith as a grain of mustard seed,* ye shall say unto this mountain, Remove hence to yonder place; and it shall remove; and nothing shall be impossible unto you (Matthew 17:20).

What Jesus meant here is that even the smallest amount of faith, *if it is genuine and placed in God,* can accomplish great things. A mustard sees is extremely small, but it grows into a plant in time.

God can take a little and make it into much!

The question is this: will a man place His faith in Christ or in some other place? This decision is crucial, for there is no other way to be saved (John 14:6; Acts 4:12).

should not perish *The ultimate panacea*
A "panacea" is a "cure all." Jesus can and has cured all kinds of diseases of the body, and He is surely the only remedy to the diseases of the soul.

Imagine that a medical researcher one day soon comes up with a great breakthrough, announcing to all that he has discovered a cure for lung cancer. It is a sure cure, and it is relatively inexpensive.

People from all over the world would be thrilled and give great honor to that man.

Jesus, however, offers a total cure that lasts forever, no matter how great the sin might be! It does not matter what the nature of the sin is, whether it was committed at a young age or an old age, or how awful man may think it is. Jesus paid for that sin, and belief in Him carries with it the promise that such a person *will not perish!* Surely God cannot lie about a matter like this!

but have *The ultimate possession*
The Greek verb here is in the present tense. This means a believer *continually* has the eternal life God offers!

everlasting life *The ultimate promise*
For hundreds, perhaps thousands of years, man has sought a "fountain of youth." Of course the efforts have failed to prolong life much, and eventually all pass away and must face God.

The promise of this verse is that the salvation that comes by faith in Christ produces *eternal life.*

The simplest way to explain the last three phrases in John 3:16 would be this: if you are genuinely saved, your eternal salvation is as sure as the promises of God—you will not perish; you have an enduring possession; God gives you eternal life! What a verse, what promises, and what a salvation! To God be for glory, for He has done this for all of us who are truly unworthy!

In this section we will consider the following subjects: assurance of salvation, ultimate sanctification, glorification, rewards, our future reign with Christ, and heaven.

I Know Whom
I Have Believed
Daniel W. Whittle

I know not why God's wondrous grace
To me He hath made known,
Nor why, unworthy, Christ in love
Redeemed me for His own.

I know not how this saving faith
To me He did impart,
Nor how believing in His Word
Wrought peace within my heart.

I know not how the Spirit moves,
Convincing men of sin,
Revealing Jesus through the Word,
Creating faith within.

But I know Whom I have believed,
And am persuaded
That He is able
To keep that which I've committed
Unto Him against that day!

XXII

Assurance

Surely goodness and mercy shall follow me all the days of my life:
and I will dwell in the house of the Lord for ever
(Psalm 23:6).

Kind David lived three thousand years ago. When he wrote Psalm 23:6 (quoted above), he was certain of two things.

First, he was sure of God's merciful provision as long as he lived on this earth.

Second, he was confident that he would live with the Lord forever.

He wrote these words in spite of the fact that he was a sinner who had committed both adultery and murder. The story of how he fell into such deep sin is recorded in II Samuel 11.

Some tend to argue that David may have lost his salvation but then regained it. This simply is not the case. What we see is that when David sinned, it was exposed, and he repented, believing God would forgive. Consider his thoughts in Psalm 51:

Against Thee, Thee only have I sinned, and done this evil in Thy sight: that Thou mightiest be justified when Thou speakest, and be clear when Thou judgest (Psalm 51:4).

Purge me with hyssop, and I shall be clean: wash me, and I shall be whiter than snow (Psalm 51:7).

Having repented, David had one major request of God:

Restore unto me the joy of Thy salvation; and uphold me with Thy free Spirit (Psalm 51:12).

Notice that he did not ask God for a restoration of salvation, but rather a restoration of the *joy* of his salvation.

Nobody would argue successfully that sin is a good thing. It breaks fellowship, causes turmoil in the lives of people, and offends God. However, when a believer sins, God acts as a loving Father Who will discipline in such a way as to restore the fellowship He so strongly desires with one of His children.

Several verses in Scripture teach the value of God's discipline. He disciplines His children as a loving Father.

For whom the Lord loveth He chasteneth, and scourges every son whom He receiveth. If ye endure chastening, God dealeth with you as with sons; for what son is he whom the father chasteneth not (Hebrews 12:6-7)?

Behold, *happy is the man whom the Lord correcteth:* therefore despise not thou the chastising of the Almighty (Job 5:17).

For he that eateth and drinketh unworthily, eateth and drinketh damnation to himself, not discerning the Lord's body. *For this cause many are weak and sickly among you, and many sleep.* For if we would judge ourselves, we should not be judged (I Corinthians 11:29-31).

As many as I love, I rebuke and chasten: be zealous therefore, and repent (Revelation (3:19).

The verses quoted above indicate very clearly that a Christian who sins will be disciplined by God. He is a good Father, and He knows what needs to be done. Although discipline is not pleasant for the believer, God knows it is necessary at times.

There is no indication, however, that discipline involves the loss of eternal life. In fact, there are many Biblical truths which demonstrate the eternal security of a true believer. The following list certainly is not exhaustive, but it should prove helpful.

I. All three Persons of the trinity are involved in a Christian's salvation.
    God the Father planned it before He created the universe. He foreknew it, He chose it, and He predestinated it. See the first three chapters of this book concerning the pre-science (planning) of our salvation.

    Jesus shed His precious blood to pay for a Christian's salvation. See the chapter on redemption.

    The Holy Spirit was and is very active in a Christian's salvation. He regenerated, sanctified, gives gifts, produces fruit, baptizes into the body of Christ, and seals all who are saved. Some of these things happen at the moment of salvation, others are ongoing processes.

    What shall we say then to these things? If God be for us, who can be against us? He that spared not His own Son, but delivered Him up for us all, how shall He not freely give us all things? Who shall lay any thing to the charge of God's elect? It is God that justifieth. *Who is he that condemneth? It is Christ that died, yea rather, that is risen again, Who is even at the right hand of God, Who also maketh intercession for us* (Romans 8:31-34).

Question: What can we (or even Satan) do to overturn the work of all three Persons of the trinity?

II. God's grace is incredibly powerful. In fact, as plenteous as our sin may be, God is able to overpower it by His grace.

Moreover the Law entered, that the offense might abound. *But where sin abounded, grace did much more abound.* That as sin hath reigned unto death, even so might grace reign through righteousness unto eternal life by Jesus Christ our Lord (Romans 5:20-21).

Christ's blood appeases the wrath of the Father.
Much more then, *being now justified by His blood, we shall be saved from wrath through Him* (Romans 5:9).

Jesus is not only the object of our faith, but the originator and finisher as well.
Looking unto Jesus the author and finisher of our faith; Who for the joy that was set before Him endured the cross, despising the shame, and is set down at the right hand of the throne of God. For consider Him that endured such contradiction of sinners against Himself... (Hebrews 12:2-3a).

God is the originator of repentance.
Or despisest thou the riches of His goodness and forbearance and longsuffering; *not knowing that the goodness of God leadeth thee to repentance* (Romans 2:4)?

God has bestowed His amazing love on His own!
Behold, what manner of love the Father hath bestowed upon us, that we should be called the sons of God: therefore, the world knoweth us not, because it knew Him not (I John 3:1).

Question: What sin can a believer commit that will change or nullify any of these great truths?

III. Consider the great promises of God regarding salvation.
God will never abandon a believer. Verses from both the Old and New Testament could be quoted here, but this will suffice:
Let your conversation be without covetousness; and be content with such things as ye have: for He hath said, *I will never leave thee, nor forsake thee.* So that we may boldly say, The Lord is my helper, and I will not fear what man shall do unto me (Hebrews 13:5-6).

God's record on a believer is eternal life.
And this is the record, that God hath given to us eternal life, and this life is in His Son (I John 5:11).

God has promised an incredible inheritance which is eternal and cannot in any way be nullified.
That in the dispensation of the fullness of times He might gather in one all things in Christ, both which are in heaven, and which are on earth; even in Him;

in Whom also we have obtained an inheritance, being predestinated according to the purpose of Him Who worketh all things after the counsel of His own will (Ephesians 1:10-11).

Blessed be the God and Father of our Lord Jesus Christ, which according to His abundant mercy hath begotten us again unto a lively hope by the resurrection of Jesus Christ from the dead, *To an inheritance incorruptible, and undefiled, and that fadeth not away, reserved in heaven for you,* Who are kept by the power of God through faith unto salvation ready to be revealed in the last time (I Peter 1:3-5).

God has promised to continue His work in salvation until the end.
Being confident of this very thing, that *He which hath begun a good work in you will perform it until the day of Jesus Christ* (Philippians 1:6).

God is in charge of the maintenance of our salvation.
Who are *kept by the power of God through faith unto salvation ready to be revealed in the last time* (I Peter 1:5).

Nothing can keep a believer from God's great love.
Who shall separate us from the love of Christ? Shall tribulation, or distress, or persecution, or famine, or nakedness, or peril, or sword? *For I am persuaded, that neither death, nor life, nor angels, nor principalities, nor powers, nor things present, nor things to come, Nor height, nor depth, nor any other creature shall be able to separate us from the love of God which is in Christ Jesus our Lord* (Romans 8:35, 38-39).

God promises a special resurrection for the believer.
For if we have been planted together in the likeness of His death, *we shall be also in the likeness of His resurrection* (Romans 6:5).

Beloved, now are we the sons of God, and it doth not yet appear what we shall be; but we know that, when He shall appear, *we shall be like Him, for we shall see Him as He is.* And every man that hath this hope in him purifieth himself, even as He is pure (I John 3:2-3).

Question: Would God actually offer these precious promises and then not deliver on them?

IV. Consider some of the great doctrines of salvation (soteriology).
In regeneration God gives new life. This new life involves total changes in every aspect of our existence.
A new heart also will I give you, and a new spirit will I put within you: and I will take away the stony heart out of your flesh, and I will give you an heart of flesh (Ezekiel 36:26).

In sanctification the Spirit makes a believer holy.
But we are bound to give thanks to God for you, brethren beloved of the Lord, because *God hath from the beginning chosen you to salvation through sanctification of the Spirit and belief of the truth:* Whereunto He called you by our Gospel, to the obtaining of the glory of our Lord Jesus Christ (II Thessalonians 2:13-14).

In justification God declares a believer to be righteous.
Therefore being justified by faith, we have peace with God through our Lord Jesus Christ (Romans 5:1).

In Spirit baptism a believer is brought into the family of God.
For by one Spirit are we all baptized into one body, whether we be Jews or Gentiles, whether we be bond or free; and have been all made to drink into one Spirit (I Corinthians 12:13).

In adoption the believer receives all the privileges of an adult son of God.
He that overcometh shall inherit all things; and I will be his God, and He shall be My son (Revelation 21:7).

The sealing of the Holy Spirit is permanent and places God's approval on salvation.
And grieve not the Holy Spirit of God, *whereby ye are sealed unto the day of redemption* (Ephesians 4:30).

In propitiation the blood of Christ removes God's wrath toward our sin.
And He is the propitiation for our sins: and not for ours only, but also for the sins of the whole world (I John 2:2).

Question: What Scripture explains how these doctrines no longer apply?

Perhaps a simple Gospel song will help conclude these thoughts:

It is Surely Sufficient for Me
Anonymous

It is surely sufficient for me,
It is surely sufficient for me.
If the blood of Christ is sufficient for God,
It is surely sufficient for me!

If somehow believers could do something to save themselves or maintain their salvation, then there would be considerable cause for concern and reasons to have doubts about the eternal life God offers. All man can do is sinful, but Jesus paid the price for all that sin!

Blessed assurance, Jesus is mine!
Oh, what a foretaste of glory Divine!
Heir of salvation, purchase of God,
Born of His Spirit,
Washed in His blood!

Perfect submission, all is at rest,
I in my Savior am happy and blest!
Watching and waiting, looking above,
Filled with His goodness,
Lost in His love!

This is my story;
This is my song;
Praising my Savior,
All the day long!

Blessed Assurance
Fanny J. Crosby

XXIII

Ultimate Sanctification

But when that which is perfect is come, then that which is in part
shall be done away (I Corinthians 13:10).

In *positional* sanctification the believer is released from the *penalty* of his sin. In *practical* sanctification the believer is gradually released from the *power* of sin in this life. In *ultimate* sanctification the believer will be eternally delivered from both the *presence* and the *possibility* of sin. This chapter will consider the subject of ultimate sanctification.

God is holy and He will live forever with those who are ultimately made holy.

Below is a list of Biblical truths about this important subject:

1. **Believers will be ultimately sanctified when Jesus comes.**
   To the end He may stablish your hearts unblameable in holiness before God, even our Father, *at the coming of our Lord Jesus Christ with all His saints* (I Thessalonians 3:13).

   So Christ was once offered to bear the sins of many; and *unto them that look for Him shall He appear the second time without sin unto salvation* (Hebrews 9:28).

   Beloved, now are we the sons of God, and it doth not yet appear what we shall be: But we know that, *when He shall appear, we shall be like Him: for we shall see Him as He is.* And every man that hath this hope in him purifieth himself, even as He is pure (I John 3:2-3).

2. **Everything will be new in the final state.**
   And He that sat upon the throne said, *Behold, I make all things new.* And He said unto me, Write: for these words are true and faithful (Revelation 21:5).

3. **The changes will be radical.**
   But when that which is perfect is come, *then that which is in part shall be done away* (I Corinthians 13:10).

   To open their eyes, *and to turn them from darkness to light, and from the power of Satan unto God,* that they may receive forgiveness of sins, and inheritance among them that are sanctified by faith that is in me (Acts 26:18).

4. **The sanctification is permanent.**
   For by one offering *hath He perfected for ever them that are sanctified* (Hebrews 10:14).

He that is unjust, let him be unjust still; and he which is filthy, let him be filthy still: *and he that is righteous, let him be righteous still: and he that is holy, let him be holy still* (Revelation 22:11).

5. **There will be absolutely no sin in heaven.**
And there shall in no wise enter any thing that defileth, neither whatsoever worketh abomination, or maketh a lie; but they which are written in the Lamb's book of life (Revelation 21:27).

6. **This total sanctification is based on the holiness of Christ's blood.**
And one of the elders answered, saying unto me, What are these which arrayed in white robes? And whence came they? And I said unto him, Sir, thou knowest. And he said to me, *These are they which came out of great tribulation, and have washed their robes, and made them white in the blood of the Lamb* (Revelation 7:14).

7. **Ultimate sanctification brings great joy to Christ.**
Now unto Him that is able to keep you from falling, and to present you faultless before the presence of His glory *with exceeding joy,* To the only wise God our Savior, be glory and majesty, dominion and power, both now and ever. Amen (Jude 24-25).

8. **Ultimate sanctification is the plan of the Father.**
Blessed be the God and Father of our Lord Jesus Christ, Who hath blessed us with all spiritual blessings in heavenly places in Christ: *According as He hath chosen us in Him before the foundation of the world, that we should be holy and without blame before Him* in love (Ephesians 1:3-4).

Sin is so prevalent in this world that it is difficult to imagine being ultimately sanctified, but that is God's promise from His Word.

To Him be the glory forever!

Holy, holy, holy!
Lord God Almighty!
Early in the morning
Our song shall rise to Thee;
Holy, holy, holy!
Merciful and mighty!
God in three Persons,
Blessed Trinity!

Holy, Holy, Holy
Reginald Heber

XXIV

Glorification

Whereunto He called you by our Gospel, to the obtaining of the glory of our Lord Jesus Christ (II Thessalonians 2:14).

The doctrine of glorification is closely related to ultimate sanctification. Obviously, anyone who has sin cannot totally glorify God; so these two doctrines must go together. It is also true that both of these great truths are reserved for the final state in heaven.

Whereas ultimate sanctification has to do with the removal of sin, glorification involves a total change in the body of believers.

For our conversation is in heaven: from whence we look for the Savior, the Lord Jesus Christ: *Who shall change our vile body, that it may be fashioned like unto His glorious body,* according to the working whereby He is able even to subdue all things unto Himself (Philippians 3:20-21).

The Hebrew and Greek words normally translated "glory" are quite interesting. The Hebrew verb *kaveth,* for instance, actually means "to weigh heavily." One might well ask what "weighing heavily" has to do with glory.

The answer lies in the fact that many precious stones are more valuable than a few, and "weighing heavily" many times has the idea of "being important."

Below are three references from the Old Testament where this interesting verb is used:

But the hand of the Lord *was heavy upon them of Ashdod,* and He destroyed them, and smote them with emerods, even Ashdod and the coasts thereof (I Samuel 5:6).

And the Lord said, Because the cry of Sodom and Gomorrah is great, and because *their sin is very grievous:* I will go down now, and see whether they have done altogether according to the cry of it... (Genesis 18:20-21a).

Poverty and shame shall be to him that refuseth instruction: but he that regardeth reproof *shall be honored* (Proverbs 13:18).

The Greek noun *doxa* generally means "opinion," but can also mean "praise, good reputation." Obviously, when used with reference to God or the final state of believers, the word means "glory."

Below is a list of references which speaks on the subject of glory in general:

1. **Creation declares the glory of God.**

The heavens declare the glory of God; and the firmament showeth his handiwork (Psalm 19:1).

2. **Sin causes man to fall short of God's glory.**
    For all have sinned, and *come short of the glory of God* (Romans 3:23).

3. **Praise and unity glorify God.**
    Now the God of patience and consolation grant you to be likeminded one toward another according to Jesus Christ: *That ye may with one mind and one mouth glorify God, even the Father of our Lord Jesus Christ. Wherefore receive ye one another, as Christ received us to the glory of God* (Romans 15:5-7).

4. **Both Jesus and the Father were glorified in Christ's death.**
    Therefore, when He was gone out, Jesus said, *Now is the Son of man glorified, and God glorified in Him.* If God be glorified in Him, God shall also glorify Him in Himself, and shall straightway glorify Him (John 13:31-32).

Below is a list of Biblical facts about the glorification of believers. What amazing changes will take place in heaven, for believers will then be beyond the possibility of ever sinning again!

1. **Believers will not become God, but they will receive the same nature He has.**
    Whereby are given unto us exceeding great and precious promises: that by these *ye might be partakers of the divine nature,* having escaped the corruption that is in the world through lust (II Peter 1:4).

2. **Believers will obtain the glory of Jesus Christ.**
    Whereunto He called you by our Gospel, *to the obtaining of the glory of our Lord Jesus Christ* (II Thessalonians 2:14).

3. **Jesus will present the Church as glorious.**
    That He might sanctify and cleanse it with the washing of water by the Word, that *He might present it to Himself a glorious church,* not having spot, or wrinkle, or any such thing; but that it should be holy and without blemish (Ephesians 5:26-27).

4. **God prepared the glorification of believers long before creation.**

    In the mind of God glorification is already an accomplished fact.

    For whom He did foreknow, He also did predestinate to be conformed to the image of His Son, that He might be the firstborn among many brethren. Moreover, whom He did predestinate, them He also called; and whom He called, them He also justified, *and whom He justified, them He also glorified* (Romans 8:29-30).

And that He might make known the riches of His glory on the vessels of mercy, *which He had afore prepared unto glory* (Romans 9:23).

The bride eyes not her garment,
But her dear Bridegroom's face:
I will not gaze at glory,
But on my King of grace—
Not at the crown He giveth,
But on His pierced hand:
The Lamb is all the glory
Of Immanuel's land!

Immanuel's Land
Ann Ross Cousin

XXV

Rewards

And every man that striveth for the mastery is temperate in all things. Now they do it to obtain a corruptible crown; but we an incorruptible (I Corinthians 9:25).

The crowns mentioned in I Corinthians 9:25 are those won by contestants who had performed well in athletic competition. Many times those crowns were made of olive branches which lasted only for a short time.

Sometimes Christians wonder if there is anything to be gained in serving God. They realize He has saved them, but will there be a bonus for such effort? And if there is one, will it soon become worthless like the crowns the ancient athletes won in their games?

The answer is that God gives rewards both in this life and in heaven:

1. **God's reward for faithfulness is praise from Him.**
   Moreover it is required in stewards that a man be found faithful. Therefore judge nothing before the time, until the Lord come, Who both will bring to light the hidden things of darkness, and will make manifest the counsels of the hearts: *and then shall every man have praise of God* (I Corinthians 4:2, 5).

2. **God gives rewards to those who make good use of the opportunities He has given.**
   At the end of the parable of the talents, Jesus said, "Take from him the pound, and give it to him that hath ten pounds. (And they said unto him, Lord, he hath ten pounds.) For I say unto you, *That every one which hath shall be given; and from him that hath not, even that which he hath shall be taken away from him*" (Luke 19:24-26; read the entire account in Luke 19:11-27).

3. **Rewards will be granted according to how much heartfelt energy is expended.**
   But this I say, *He which soweth sparingly shall reap also sparingly; and he which soweth bountifully shall also reap bountifully* (II Corinthians 9:6).

4. **Those who are wise in God's eyes will shine as the stars.**
   And many of them that sleep in the dust of the earth shall awake, some to everlasting life, and some to shame and everlasting contempt. *And they that be wise shall shine as the brightness of the firmament;* and they that turn many to righteousness as the stars for ever and ever (Daniel 12:2-3).

5. **God rewards the doing of good whether it is something large or small.**
   And let us not grow weary in well doing: *for in due season we shall reap if we faint not.* As we have therefore opportunity, let us do good unto all men, especially unto them who are of the household of faith (Galatians 6:9-10).

He that receiveth you receiveth Me, and he that receiveth Me receiveth Him that sent Me. He that receiveth a prophet in the name of a prophet shall receive a prophet's reward; and he that receiveth a righteous man in the name of a righteous man shall receive a righteous man's reward. *And whosoever shall give to drink of these little ones a cup of cold water only in the name of a disciple, verily I say unto you, he shall in no wise lose his reward* (Matthew 10:40-42).

6. **God will give rewards to those who have suffered for Him.**
Blessed are ye, when men shall revile you, and persecute you, and shall say all manner of evil against you falsely, for My sake. Rejoice, and be exceeding glad: *for great is your reward in heaven: for so persecuted they the prophets which were before you* (Matthew 5:11-12).

7. **God will give a crown of life to those who love Him, enduring temptation.**
Blessed is the man that endureth temptation: for when he is tried, *he shall receive the crown of life, which the Lord hath promised to them that love Him* (James 1:12).

8. **God will give a crown of righteousness to those who love His appearing.**
Henceforth there is laid up for me a crown of righteousness, which the Lord, the righteous judge shall give me at that day: and not to me only, but unto all them that love His appearing (II Timothy 4:8).

9. **God will give spiritual leaders a crown of glory if they have been faithful**
Neither as being lords over God's heritage, but being examples to the flock. And when the chief Shepherd shall appear, *ye shall receive a crown of glory that fadeth not away* (I Peter 5:3-4).

10. **God gives rewards based on both His love and justice.**
See Deuteronomy 7:9-13; II Chronicles 6:14-16.

So that a man shall say, Verily *there is a reward for the righteous: verily He is a God that judgeth in the earth* (Psalm 58:11).

11. **God promises to give rewards when He comes again.**
And behold, *I come quickly; and My reward is with Me,* to give to every man according as his work shall be (Revelation 22:12).

Let us not grow weary
In the work of love,
Send the light!
Send the light!

Let us gather jewels
For a crown above,
Send the light!
Send the light!

Send the light,
The blessed Gospel light!
Let it shine
From shore to shore!
Send the light,
The blessed Gospel light,
Let it shine
For evermore!

Send the Light
Charles H. Gabriel

XXVI

Reigning with Christ

If we suffer, we shall also reign with Him (II Timothy 2:12a).

Eschatology is the doctrine of the last things. It is an important area to study, but it is also quite difficult. Some things about prophecy are clear:

The church will be raptured, there will be a tribulation period of seven years, there will be a great battle called Armageddon, there will be a millennium, there will be a brief final battle after the millennium, and there will be a literal heaven and hell in the final state.

There are some things about prophecy which are not clear:

When will the rapture take place? Who is the antichrist? Where exactly will anti-christ's Babylon be? Some say it will be in Rome because of the seven hills mentioned in Revelation 17:9, but by that time in the tribulation period the entire earth's landscape will be so radically changed, who knows where those seven hills will be?

The subject of reigning with Christ seems to be twofold. "Seems" is the operative word, because the subject gets a bit complicated at times.

Anyhow, the first aspect of reigning with Christ will take place during the millennium (that one thousand year period during which He will live on and rule the earth); the second aspect of reigning with Him is in the final state.

The discussion of this subject will be divided into three sections.

1. **There are some references in which the time of reigning with Christ is not clear. These may be millennial or eternal.**
    Suffering saints will rule with Christ.
    If we suffer, we shall also reign with Him (II Timothy 2:12a).

    Saints will judge angels.
    Know ye not that we shall judge angels? How much more things that pertain to this life (I Corinthians 6:3)?

    Saints will judge the world.
    Do ye not know that the saints will judge the world? And if the world shall be judged by you, are ye unworthy to judge the smallest matters (I Corinthians 6:2)?

2. **There are some references in which the time of the reigning with Christ seems to be during the millennium.**

And he that overcometh, and keepeth my works unto the end, to him will I give power over the nations: *And He shall rule them with a rod of iron;* as the vessels of a potter shall they be broken to shivers: even as I received of My Father (Revelation 2:26-27).

Those who are faithful to Christ during the tribulation will reign with Him during the millennium.
And I saw thrones, and they that sat on them, and judgment was given unto them: *And I saw the souls of them that were beheaded for the witness of Jesus,* and for the Word of God, and which had not worshipped the beast, neither his image, neither had received his mark upon their foreheads, or in their hands; *and they lived and reigned with Christ a thousand years* (Revelation 20:6).

Jerusalem will be the capital.
And it shall come to pass in the last days, that the mountain of the Lord's house shall be established in the top of the mountains, and shall be exalted above the hills; and all nations shall flow into it. And many people shall go and say, Come ye, and let us go up to the mountain of the Lord, to the house of the God of Jacob; and He will teach us of His ways. And we will walk in His paths: *for out of Zion shall go forth the law, and the Word of the Lord from Jerusalem* (Isaiah 2:2-3).

3. **There are some references in which the time of the reigning with Christ is clearly eternal.**
The nations and kings of the earth will honor the new Jerusalem.
And the city had no need of the sun, neither of the moon, to shine in it: for the glory of God did lighten it, and the Lamb is the light thereof. And the nations of them which are saved shall walk in the light of it: *and the kings of the earth do bring their glory and honor into it* (Revelation 21:23-24).

The idea of nations, kings, and people living on the earth forever seems to be a fulfillment of Isaiah 9:6-7. The interpretation goes something like this: since there will be people who will live through the millennium who were saved and faithful to Christ all those years, they will be the ones who will have children on into eternity. Notice it says in verse 7, "of the increase of His government there shall be no end." By combining this with what we know in Revelation, we reach this probable conclusion.

For unto us a child is born, unto us a son is given: and the government shall be upon His shoulder: and His name shall be called Wonderful, Counselor, the mighty God, the everlasting Father, the Prince of Peace. *Of the increase of His government there shall be no end,* upon the throne of David, and upon His Kingdom, to order it, and to establish it with judgment and justice from henceforth even for ever. The zeal of the Lord of hosts will perform this (Isaiah 9:6-7).

Jews who have been saved will play a role in reigning with Christ.
I have made a covenant with My chosen, I have sworn unto David My servant, Thy seed will I establish forever, and build thy throne to all generations. Selah (Psalm 89:3-4).

Jesus will reign from His own throne forever.
He shall be great, and shall be called the Son of the Highest: and the Lord God shall give unto Him the throne of his father David: *and He shall reign over the house of Jacob for ever:* and of His kingdom there shall be no end (Luke 1:31-32).

The apostles will rule over the twelve tribes of Israel.
Then answered Peter and said unto Him, Behold, we have forsaken all, and followed Thee; what shall we have therefore? And Jesus said unto them, Verily I say unto you, That ye which have followed Me, in the regeneration when the Son of man shall sit in the throne of His glory, *ye also shall sit upon twelve thrones, judging the twelve tribes of Israel* (Matthew 19:27-28).

Obviously God honors those who honor Him, so we would do well to be obedient. The rewards are spectacular and there are eternal positions available!

Jesus Shall Reign
Isaac Watts

Jesus shall reign
Wheree're the sun
Does his successive journeys run;
His kingdom spread
From shore to shore,
Till moons shall wax
And wane no more.

Victory Through Grace
Fanny J. Crosby

Conquering now and still to conquer,
Jesus, Thou ruler of all.
Thrones and their scepters
All shall perish,
Crowns and their splendor shall fall;
Yet shall the armies Thou leadest,
Faithful and true to the last,
Find in Thy mansions eternal
Rest, when their warfare is past!

Not to the strong is the battle,
Not to the swift is the race,
Yet to the true and the faithful
Victory is promised through grace!

XXVII

Heaven

For, behold, I create new heavens and a new earth: and the former shall not be remembered, nor come into mind (Isaiah 65:17).

Many great hymns and Gospel songs have been written about heaven. No doubt many Christians can confidently agree with these thoughts:

For here have we no continuing city, *but we seek one to come* (Hebrews 13:14).

This being so, we long to see Jesus and our loved ones! In addition, we will spend eternity there! Just what will heaven be like? Below is a list which will give us at least some picture of its glories:

1. **There are a number of things which will not be in heaven.**
   There will be no sea (Revelation 21:1), no tears, death, sorrow, crying, or pain (Revelation 21:4), no temple (Revelation 21:22), no sun (Revelations 21:23), no gates which are shut (Revelation 21:25), no night (Revelation 21:25), no sin (Revelation 21:27), no curse (Revelation 22:3), no Satan (Revelation 20:7-10), and no time, because there will be no way to measure it or need to do so!

2. **The old heaven and earth will be burned up, and God will create new ones.**
   But the day of the Lord will come as a thief in the night; in the which *the heavens shall pass away with a great noise, and the elements shall melt with fervent heat, the earth and the works that are therein shall be burned up.* Seeing then that all these things shall be dissolved, what manner of persons ought ye to be in all conversation and godliness, Looking for and hasting unto the coming of the day of God, wherein the heavens being on fire shall be dissolved, and the elements shall melt with fervent heat (II Peter 3:10-12)?

   And I saw the new heavens and the new earth, *for the first heaven and the first earth were passed away;* and there was no more sea (Revelation 21:1).

   For as the new heavens and the new earth, which I will make, shall remain before Me, saith the Lord, so shall your seed and your name remain (Isaiah 66:22).

3. **A new Jerusalem, our new home, will be suspended between heaven and earth.**
   And I John saw the holy city, new Jerusalem, coming down from God out of heaven, prepared as a bride adorned for her husband (Revelation 21:2).

   And he carried me away in the Spirit to a great and high mountain, and showed me that great city, *the holy Jerusalem, descending out of heaven from God* (Revelation 21:10).

4. ***We will be with God the Father Himself.***
And I heard a great voice out of heaven saying, Behold, the tabernacle of God is with men, and He will dwell with them, and they shall be His people, *and God Himself shall be with them, and be their God* (Revelation 21:3).

5. ***We will be with our Savior Jesus Christ.***
And there shall be no more curse: *but the throne of God and of the Lamb shall be in it;* and His servants shall serve Him: And they shall see His face; and His name shall be in their foreheads (Revelation 22:3-4).

6. ***Heaven is eternal.***
And there shall be no more night there; and they need no candle, neither light of the sun; for the Lord God giveth them light; *and they shall reign for ever and ever* (Revelation 22:5).

7. ***Heaven is a beautiful place.***
Revelation 21:11-21 mentions precious stones, pure gold, and huge pearl gates.

8. ***The new Jerusalem will be a large city (probably cubed in shape).***
And he that talked with me had a golden reed to measure the city, and the gates thereof, and the wall thereof. And the city lieth foursquare, and the length is as large as the breadth: and he measured the city with the reed, *twelve thousand furlongs.* The length and the breadth and the height of it are equal (Revelation 21:16).

9. ***There will be pure water in heaven.***
And he showed me *a pure river of water of life, clear as crystal,* proceeding out of the throne of God and of the Lamb (Revelation 22:1).

10. ***There will be a tree of life in heaven.***
In the midst of the street of it, and on either side of the river, *was there the tree of life,* which bare twelve manner of fruits, and yielded her fruit every month: and the leaves of the tree were for the healing of the nations (Revelation 22:2).

11. ***Heaven could be ours today because His return is imminent!***
And he said unto me, These things are faithful and true: and the Lord God of the holy prophets sent His angel to show unto His servants the things which must shortly be done. *Behold, I come quickly:* blessed is he that keepeth the sayings of the prophecy of this book (Revelation 22:6-7).

12. ***Jesus instructed us about heaven and His role in its preparation.***
In My Father's house are many mansions: if it were not so, I would have told you. *I go to prepare a place for you.* And if I go and prepare a place for you, I will come again, and receive you unto myself: that where I am there ye may be also (John 14:2-3).

13. **There will be thrones in heaven for both the Father and the Son.**
...but the throne of God and of the Lamb shall be in it (Revelation 22:3b).

14. **We will serve God in heaven.**
...and His servants shall serve Him (Revelation 22:3c).

15. **There will be a great number of redeemed souls in heaven.**
After this I beheld, and, lo, *a great multitude, which no man can number,* of all nations, and kindreds, and people, and tongues, stood before the throne, and before the Lamb, clothed with white robes, and palms in their hands (Revelation 7:9-10).

And I say unto you, That *many shall come from the east and the west,* and shall sit down with Abraham, and Isaac, and Jacob, in the kingdom of heaven (Matthew 8:11).

To conclude these thoughts, surely we can say with the Apostle Paul,

O the depth of the riches both of the wisdom and knowledge of God! How unsearchable are His judgments, and His ways past finding out (Romans 11:33)!

When We All Get to Heaven
Eliza E. Hewitt

Sing the wondrous love of Jesus,
Sing His mercy and His grace;
In the mansions bright and blessed,
He'll prepare for us a place.

Let us then be true and faithful,
Trusting, serving every day:
Just one glimpse of Him in glory
Will the toils of life repay!

When we all get to heaven,
What a day of rejoicing that will be!
When we all see Jesus,
We'll sing and shout the victory!

Section IV: The Practicality of Our Salvation
Overview

How precious also are Thy thoughts unto me, O God! How great is the sum of them (Psalm 139:17)!

Sometimes in the Christian walk it is very helpful to take time to just ponder God's goodness. David understood this when he wrote,

He maketh me to lie down in green pastures: He leadeth me beside the still waters (Psalm 23:2).

In this overview, please ponder this list of amazing truths about our salvation:

1. **The Immortal died.**
   Jesus, the eternal Son of God (John 1:1), actually died (Luke 23:46).

2. **The sovereign Creator became a mere human, maintaining His deity.**
   And the Word was made flesh, and dwelt among us, (and we beheld His glory, the glory as of the only begotten of the Father,) full of grace and truth (John 1:14).

3. **He Who hates sin died for the salvation of sinners.**
   For scarcely for a righteous man will one die; yet peradventure for a good man some would even dare to die. *But God commendeth His love toward us, in that, while we were yet sinners, Christ died for us* (Romans 5:7-8).

4. **Satan, our powerful spiritual father before salvation, is now our easily defeated enemy.**
   Submit yourselves therefore to God. *Resist the devil, and he will flee from you* (James 4:7).

5. **We who were once God's enemies are now His close friends.**
   And the Scripture was fulfilled which saith, Abraham believed God, and it was imputed unto him for righteousness: *and he was called the Friend of God* (James 2:23).

6. **Jesus came into His own creation, yet His own people would not receive Him.**
   He came unto His own, and His own received Him not (John 1:11).

7. **As awful as our sins were and are, God's grace is able to overcome it easily.**
   Moreover the Law entered, that the offense might abound. *But where sin abounded, grace did much more abound* (Romans 5:20).

8. **Our mortal bodies will receive immortality.**
   For this corruptible must put on incorruption, and this mortal must put on

immortality. So when this corruptible shall have put on incorruption, and this mortal shall have put on immortality, then shall be brought to pass that is written, Death is swallowed up in victory. O death, where is thy sting? O grave, where is thy victory (I Corinthians 15:53-55)?

Paul expands on this more in the same chapter:
There is one glory of the sun, and another glory of the moon, and another glory of the stars: for one star differeth from another star in glory. So also is the resurrection of the dead. *It is sown in corruption; it is raised in incorruption:* It is sown in dishonor; it is raised in glory: it is sown in weakness; it is raised in power (I Corinthians 15:41-43).

9. *He Who is our High Priest also offered Himself as our sacrifice.*

So also Christ glorified not Himself to be made an high priest; but He that said unto Him, Thou art My Son, today I have begotten Thee, As He saith in another place, Thou art a priest for ever after the order of Melchisedek (Hebrews 5:5-6).

But Christ, being come an high priest of good things to come, by a greater and more perfect tabernacle, not made with hands, that is to say, not of this building; neither by the blood of goats and calves, *but by His own blood He entered in once into the holy place, having obtained eternal redemption for us.* For if the blood of bulls and goats, and the ashes of an heifer sprinkling the unclean, sanctifieth to the purification of the flesh: How much more shall the blood of Christ, Who through the eternal Spirit offered Himself without spot to God, purge your conscience from dead works to serve the living God (Hebrews 9:11-14)?

10. *The omnipotent God, Who strictly demands our worship of Him alone, humbled Himself even to the death of the cross.*

Let this mind be in you, which was also in Christ Jesus: Who, being in the form of God, thought it not robbery to be equal with God: but made Himself of no reputation, and took upon Him the form of a servant, and was made in the likeness of men: And being found in fashion as a man, *He humbled Himself, and became obedient unto death, even the death of the cross* (Philippians 2:5-8).

11. *For a believer, success in this life must involve death to self.*

And he that taketh not his cross, and followeth after Me, is not worthy of Me. He that findeth his life shall lose it: and *he that loseth his life for My sake shall find it.* He that receiveth you receiveth Me, and he that receiveth Me receiveth Him that sent Me (Matthew 10:38-40).

I beseech you therefore, brethren, by the mercies of God, *that ye present your bodies a living sacrifice,* holy, acceptable unto God, which is your reasonable service. And be not conformed to this world: but be ye transformed by the renewing of your mind, that ye may prove what is that good, and acceptable, and perfect, will of God (Romans 12:1-2).

I am crucified with Christ: nevertheless I live; yet not I, but Christ liveth in me: and the life that I now live in the flesh I live by the faith of the Son of God, Who loved me, and gave Himself for me (Galatians 2:20).

12. Even though we are at best sinners saved by grace, God has given us responsible positions and all we need to be successful in them.
He has given us gifts and the fruit of the Spirit so that we can capably serve as a priest and an ambassador.

13. The omnipotent and sinless Holy Spirit now continually indwells the bodies of sinners saved by grace. Furthermore, He considers those bodies the holiest of places.
What? Know ye not that *your body is the temple of the Holy Ghost which is in you,* which ye have of God, and ye are not your own? For ye are bought with a price; therefore glorify God in your body, and in your spirit, which are God's (I Corinthians 6:19-20).

14. He Who is angry at man's sin provided the propitiation for man's sin.
And He is the propitiation for our sins: and not for ours only, but also for the sins of the whole world (I John 2:2).

We would do well to ponder God's goodness to us often!

Here are some fitting words from the Apostle Paul.

Finally, brethren, whatsoever things are true, whatsoever things are honest, whatsoever things are just, whatsoever things are pure, whatsoever things are of good report; *if there be any virtue, and if there be any praise, think on these things.* Those things, which ye have both learned, and received, and heard, and seen in me, do: and the God of peace shall be with you (Philippians 4:8-9).

To God be the glory,
Great things He hath done,
So loved He the world
That He gave us His Son,
Who yielded His life,
An atonement for sin,
And opened the Lifegate
That all may go in.

O perfect redemption,
The purchase of blood,
To every believer
The promise of God;
The vilest offender
Who truly believes
That moment from Jesus
A pardon receives!

Praise the Lord, praise the Lord,
Let the earth hear His voice!
Praise the Lord, praise the Lord,
Let the people rejoice!
O come to the Father
Through Jesus, the Son,
And give Him the glory,
Great things He hath done!

To God be the Glory
Fanny J. Crosby

XXVIII

The Role of the Law

For the Law, having a shadow of good things to come, and not the very image of the things, can never with those sacrifices which they offered year by year continually make the comers thereunto perfect (Hebrews 10:1).

Man has had law codes for thousands of years. Probably the earliest example is the famous code of Hammurabi from the 18th century B.C. God gave the Law to Moses in the 15th century B.C.

The purpose of all these laws is to create order in society and to discipline those who break the rules. Sometimes man's laws become oppressive; sometimes they are lax.

In the case of the Decalogue (the Ten Commandments), God made the rules, not man. Moses simply wrote in the Bible what God inspired him to write.

This gives the Old Testament Law considerable significance, especially when it comes to matters of morality.

Today most serious students of the Old Testament Law believe it has three aspects: ceremonial, civil, and moral. A brief overview of these three aspects will be given here:

A. Ceremonial.
This aspect of the Law covers such things as offerings (Leviticus 1-7), the priesthood (Leviticus 8-10), and purity (Leviticus 11-15). These regulations were in force for an amount of time specified by God.

B. Civil.
This aspect of the Law covers such things as crimes against society, property rights, military policy, and treatment of animals. These regulations can be found all throughout the books of Exodus-Numbers and were in force for an amount of time specified by God.

C. Moral.
This aspect of the Law is given in the Ten Commandments (Exodus 20:3-17; Deuteronomy 5:7-21). All of these commandments are repeated again in the New Testament (either directly or in principle) with the exception of the Sabbath.

Questions come up concerning the similarities and differences between the Old and New Testament.

In these times that which was symbolized by the Passover and circumcision came to be represented by the Lord's Supper and baptism. Concerning the sacrifice, Old

Testament saints looked forward to the ultimate sacrifice to come when they observed the Passover; New Testament saints look back at the ultimate sacrifice that Christ offered on the cross when they observe the Lord's Supper.

Regarding circumcision and baptism, there are similarities and differences. In both cases God commanded that they be done as a matter of obedience. In both cases it was clear that they did not give salvation to the people who observed them. Differences? Circumcision was to be done on the eighth day (Philippians 3:5); baptism is to be observed after receiving Christ as Savior (Acts 16:30-33).

The cross replaced the brazen altar. The "prayers of the saints" (Revelation 5:8) replaced the altar of incense. Total surrender self sacrifices offered by believers today (resulting in Spirit-filled living) have replaced the golden candlestick. Christ is now the propitiation; in Old Testament times it was a mercy seat.

The Old Testament regulations were quite cumbersome. Believers in those days had to approach a priest who would then offer an animal as a sacrifice. There was also the disadvantage of having to *wait* or *look forward to* the deliverance that would come.

Some today seem to believe that God's standards under the Law were stricter than they are under grace today, but that surely is not true:

Ye have heard that it was said by them of old time, Thou shalt not kill; and whosoever shall kill shall be in danger of judgment: But I say unto you, That *whosoever is angry with his brother without a cause shall be in danger of the judgment: and whosoever shall say to his brother, Raca, shall be in danger of the council: but whosoever shall say, Thou fool, shall be in danger of hell fire* (Matthew 5:21-22).

All these things having been said, what is the role of the Old Testament Law today? A brief list is given below:

1. **It was NEVER intended to save.**
   Knowing that a man is not justified by the works of the Law, but by the faith of Jesus Christ, even we have believed in Jesus Christ, that we might be justified by the faith of Christ. And not by the works of the Law: for by the works of the Law shall no flesh be justified (Galatians 2:16).

2. **It shows man that he cannot live up to God's standards.**
   Now we know that what things soever the Law saith, it saith to them who are under the Law: that every mouth be stopped, *and all the world may become guilty before God.* Therefore by the deeds of the Law there shall no flesh be justified in His sight: for by the Law is the knowledge of sin. But now the righteousness of God without the Law is manifested , being witnessed by the Law and the prophets; Even the righteousness of God which is by faith of Jesus Christ unto all and upon all them that believe (Romans 3:19-22a).

3. *It is God's tool to bring people to Christ.*
But before faith came, we were kept under the Law, shut up unto the faith which should afterward be revealed. *Wherefore the Law was our schoolmaster to bring us unto Christ,* that we might be justified by faith. But after that faith is come, we are no longer under a schoolmaster (Galatians 3:23-25).

The Greek noun translated "schoolmaster" is *paidagogos.* This particular word is quite interesting.

In the Greek papyri and other ancient literature it has been discovered that in many cases a *paidagogos* was a highly educated slave. When the owner of the estate wanted to send his son to a good school (often quite a distance from his home), he would entrust the care of his son to that educated, trustworthy slave.

Instructors would give their lessons, but the *paidagogos* would make sure that discipline would be administered when it was needed. For all intents and purposes, this slave was the one who was to make sure the boy did what he was supposed to do.

This is exactly the role of the Law. It shows us that we are sinful. It points us toward the grace of God when we realize we cannot save ourselves. This is what is meant by the phrase "our schoolmaster brings us unto Christ." Just as the slave made sure the boy did what he was supposed to do, the Law, properly understood and applied, brings us to our Savior!

4. *It is good if it is used as God intended.*
But we know that the Law is good, if a man use it lawfully; Knowing this, that the Law is not made for a righteous man, but for the lawless and disobedient, for the ungodly and sinners, for unholy and profane, for murderers of mothers, for manslayers, For whoremongers, for them that defile themselves with mankind, for menstealers, for liars, for perjured persons, and if there be any other thing that is contrary to sound doctrine; According to the glorious gospel of the blessed God which was committed to my trust (I Timothy 1:8-10).

As long as it is made clear that the Law never did and never can save; that it is an important part of morality for us today; and that it can and should bring us to the place of repentance, then these are good uses of the Law.

Despite the clear Biblical teachings to the contrary and the exhortations of many that we cannot save ourselves, there are still quite a number of people who are convinced that they can be saved by keeping the Law or living their version of a moral life.

This was a problem in Paul's day. There were false teachers who had perverted the Gospel message, suggesting that salvation was accomplished by circumcision and strict observance of the Law. The Apostle wasted very few words in dealing with this issue.

I marvel that ye are so soon removed from Him that called you into the grace of Christ unto another Gospel: Which is not another; but there be some that trouble you, and would pervert the Gospel of Christ. But though we, or an angel from heaven, preach any other Gospel unto you than that which we have preached unto you, let him be accursed. As we said before, so say I now again, If any man preach any other Gospel unto you than that ye have received, let him be accursed (Galatians 1:6-9).

Other verses make the point clear as well:

For what the Law could not do, in that it was weak through the flesh, God sending His own Son in the likeness of sinful flesh, and for sin, condemned sin in the flesh (Romans 8:3).

For Christ is the end of the Law for righteousness to every one that believeth (Romans 10:4).

Free from the Law,
O happy condition,
Jesus hath bled,
And there is remission;
Cursed by the Law
And bruised by the fall,
Grace has redeemed us
Once for all!

Once for all,
O sinner, receive it;
Once for all,
O brother believe it;
Cling to the cross,
The burden will fall,
Christ hath redeemed us
Once for all!

Once for All
Philip P.Bliss

XXIX

Grace

For the Lord God is a sun and shield; the Lord will give grace and glory: no good thing will He withhold from them that walk uprightly
(Psalm 84:11).

There are reasons why there are a number of hymns and Gospel songs about God's grace. It is simply amazing! Why would God care for sinners who have totally rejected Him? How can God's servants continue to labor for Him in spite of debilitating physical problems? How can a believer who doesn't have much education or experience serve His Savior? What helps us to go through really difficult challenges?

Grace! There simply isn't any other good answer!

The Greek noun for "grace" is *charis.* Its basic meaning is "a favor, gift, kindness, grace." Religion teaches that man has to "do something" in order to be saved. "Something" could include anything from helping the poor to being baptized. God makes it clear that salvation is by His grace and that He is to get the glory when one is born again. As was pointed out earlier in this book, if a man somehow could do something to save himself, then he (not He) would get the glory.

Here is a partial list of how this word "grace" is used in the New Testament:

1. *God's grace is multi-faceted.*
   As every man hath received the gift, even so minister the same one to another, *as good stewards of the manifold grace of God* (I Peter 4:10).

2. *God's grace helps believers overcome obstacles in their lives.*
   And lest I should be exalted above measure through the abundance of the revelations, there was given to me a thorn in the flesh, the messenger of Satan to buffet me, lest I should be exalted above measure. For this thing I besought the Lord thrice, that it might depart from me. And He said unto me, *My grace is sufficient for thee: for My strength is made perfect in weakness. Most gladly therefore will I rather glory in my infirmities, that the power of Christ may rest upon me* (II Corinthians 12:7-9).

3. *God shows "common grace" to all men, saved or unsaved.*
   ...for He maketh His sun to rise on the evil and on the good, and sendeth rain on the just and on the unjust (Matthew 5:45b).

4. *God's saving grace gives the believer new life.*
   Even when we were dead in sins, hath quickened us together with Christ (by grace ye are saved)—Ephesians 2:5.

5. ***God gives special grace when it is most needed.***
Let us therefore come boldly unto the throne of grace, that we may obtain mercy, *and find grace to help in time of need* (Hebrews 4:16).

6. ***Grace is the foundation of our position in Christ.***
Therefore being justified by faith, we have peace with God through our Lord Jesus Christ: *By Whom we have access by faith into this grace wherein we stand,* and rejoice in hope of the glory of God (Romans 5:1-2).

That He would grant you, according to the riches of His glory, *to be strengthened with might by His Spirit in the inner man* (Ephesians 3:16).

7. ***God gives grace so believers can do what is right.***
And God is able to make all grace abound toward you; that ye, always having all sufficiency in all things, *may abound to every good work* (II Corinthians 9:8).

8. ***God gave grace to the early church so it could grow spiritually and numerically.***
And with great power gave the apostles witness of the resurrection of the Lord Jesus: *and great grace was upon them all* (Acts 4:33).

9. ***God's grace is crucial to justification.***
Being justified freely by His grace through the redemption that is in Christ Jesus (Romans 3:24).

10. ***God's grace is the basis of His election.***
Even so then at this present time also there is a remnant *according to the election of grace* (Romans 11:5).

11. ***God's grace supplies knowledge to the believer.***
That in every thing *ye are enriched by Him, in all utterance, and in all knowledge* (I Corinthians 1:5).

12. ***God's grace helps believers overcome a shameful past.***
For I am the least of the apostles, *that I am not meet to be called an apostle, because I persecuted the church of God. But by the grace of God I am what I am:* and His grace which was bestowed upon me was not in vain; but I labored more abundantly than they all: yet not I, but the grace of God which was with me. Therefore whether it were I or they, so we preach, and so ye believed (I Corinthians 15:9-11).

And I thank Christ Jesus our Lord, Who hath enabled me, for that He counted me faithful, putting me into the ministry; Who was before a blasphemer, and a persecutor, and injurious: but I obtained mercy, because I did it ignorantly in unbelief (I Timothy 1:12-13).

13. God's grace leads to eternal glory.

But the God of all grace, Who hath called us unto His eternal glory by Christ Jesus, after that ye have suffered a while, make you perfect, stablish, strengthen, settle you (I Peter 5:10).

14. Christians are admonished to grow in grace.

But grow in grace, and in the knowledge of our Lord and Savior Jesus Christ. To Him be glory both now and for ever. Amen (II Peter 3:18).

15. Jesus was full of grace.

And the Word was made flesh, and dwelt among us, (and we beheld His glory, the glory as of the only begotten of the Father,) *full of grace and truth* (John 1:14).

16. God promises grace to the humble.

Likewise, ye younger, submit yourselves unto the elder. Yea, all of you be subject one to another, and be clothed with humility: *for God resisteth the proud, and giveth grace to the humble* (I Peter 5:5).

17. God's grace overpowers our sin!

Moreover, the Law entered, that the offense might abound. *But where sin abounded, grace did much more abound* (Romans 5:20).

18. Grace is the means of our faith.

And when he was disposed to pass through Achaia, the brethren wrote, exhorting the disciples to receive him; who, when he was come, *helped them much which had believed through grace* (Acts 18:27).

19. The New Testament covenant of grace replaced the Law.

For sin shall not have dominion over you; *for ye are not under the Law, but under grace* (Romans 6:14).

20. God's grace gives us every reason to hope in eternal life.

That being justified by His grace, we should be made heirs according to the hope of eternal life (Titus 3:7).

Here are three simple definitions of God's great grace:

"Unmerited favor."

"God's riches at Christ's expense."

"God's love and goodness extended to those who do not deserve it."

Marvelous grace of our loving Lord,
Grace that exceeds our sin and our guilt,
Yonder on Calvary's mount outpoured,
There where the blood of the Lamb was spilt.

Sin and despair like the sea waves cold,
Threaten the soul with infinite loss;
Grace that is greater, yes grace untold,
Points to the Refuge, the mighty cross!

Grace, grace, God's grace,
Grace that will pardon and cleanse within;
Grace, grace, God's grace,
Grace that is greater than all our sin!

Grace Greater than
Our Sin
Julia H. Johnston

XXX

Faith

But without faith it is impossible to please Him: for he that cometh to God must believe that He is, and that He is a rewarder of them that diligently seek Him (Hebrews 11:6).

There are some who feel that faith is simply an *emotional* response to God, having nothing to do with a person's mind or will. This author once heard a message about the resurrection of our Lord in which the speaker suggested something like this:

It really doesn't matter whether or not Jesus actually rose from the grave. What matters is that we *believe* He did.

Such preaching totally undermines the truth of the Bible and its teaching on what faith really is.

God wants us to understand that faith is based on evidence:

Now faith *is the substance of things hoped for, the evidence of things not seen.* For by it the elders obtained a good report. Through faith we understand that the worlds were framed by the word of God, so that things which are seen were not made of things which do appear (Hebrews 11:1-3).

This passage is saying that we can believe certain things because God has demonstrated His trustworthiness in the past. The reason, for instance, we can believe God will help in the future is because He has helped in the past.

That past help is *evidence* and *substance;* the trust that God will help in the future is *faith* which is based on the evidence and substance.

A close study of the Scriptures reveals that faith has three essential elements: intellectual, emotional, and volitional.

1.   *Intellectual.*
It is extremely difficult to really believe in something when you don't know what it is. Imagine trying to have a really close relationship with a person whose name you've never known and you really know virtually nothing about them! How could you honestly say you *trust* such a person? The intellectual aspect of faith is certainly not *all* there is to faith, but it should not be ignored. Below are some references which present a case for this element to saving faith:

So then *faith cometh by hearing, and hearing by the Word of God* (Romans 10:17).

Because *that which may be known of God is manifest in them; for God hath shown it unto them.* For the invisible things of Him from the creation of the world are clearly seen, being understood by the things that are made, even His eternal power and Godhead; so that they are without excuse (Romans 1:19-20).

How then shall they call on Him in Whom they have not believed? *And how shall they believe in Him of Whom they have not heard?* And how shall they hear without a preacher (Romans 10:14)?

And they that know Thy name will put their trust in Thee: for Thou, Lord, hast not forsaken them that seek Thee (Psalm 9:10).

But he that received seed into the good ground is he that heareth the Word, and understandeth it; which also beareth fruit, and bringeth forth, some an hundredfold, some sixty, some thirty (Matthew 13:23).

2. *Emotional.*

There is little doubt that emotions *do* play a role in saving faith, but it must also be said that emotions change often and easily. It is but one part of the equation.

Then believed they His words; *they sang His praise* (Psalm 106:12). Here is a verse that speaks of the emotional element of faith, but notice the potential pitfalls of depending totally on emotions:

They soon forgot His works; they waited not for His counsel: But lusted exceedingly in the wilderness, and tempted God in the desert. And He gave them their request; but sent leanness into their soul (Psalm 106:13-15).

Matthew 13:20 speaks of those who hear the Word and receive it "with joy." Such an emotion can be a sign of genuine faith, but it can also be purely unproductive emotion. Notice verse 21 of the same chapter:

Yet hath he not root in himself, but dureth for a while: for when tribulation or persecution ariseth because of the Word, by and by he is offended (Matthew 13:21).

3. *Volitional.*

This is the battle that often takes place in the will of a hearer. What will he/she *decide to do* with what they have heard? Are they willing to trust in Christ *alone* for their salvation? Are they willing to serve Him as He gives the courage, grace, and opportunity? Again, man is not saved by good works, but he is a new creature when he is saved, and he will produce fruit because he is saved!

Come unto Me, all ye that labor and are heavy laden, and I will give you rest,

Take My yoke upon you, and learn of Me; for I am meek and lowly in heart: and ye shall find rest for your souls (Matthew 11:28-29).

Unless you eat the flesh of the Son of man and drink His blood, you have no life in yourselves. He who eats My flesh and drinks My blood has eternal life; and I will raise him up at the last day (John 6:53-54, NASV).

The Bible has quite a bit to say about faith and its importance. Here are some of the highlights:

1. ***Where we place our faith is crucial.***
   For God so loved the world, that He gave His only begotten Son, that *whosoever believeth in Him* should not perish, but have everlasting life (John 3:16).

   "In Him" salvation is real; in anything or anyone else, faith is worthless!

2. ***Real faith, accompanied by a servant's attitude, pleases God.***
   By faith Enoch was translated that he should not see death; and was not found, because God translated him: for before his translation he had this testimony, *that he pleased God* (Hebrews 11:5).

3. ***Abel's sacrifice was excellent because it showed a faith that was obedient to God.***
   By faith Abel offered unto God a more excellent sacrifice than Cain, by which he obtained witness that he was righteous, God testifying of his gifts... (Hebrews 11:4a).

4. ***Abraham's faith was characterized by a willingness to do difficult things.***
   First, he was willing to leave his place of residence, not knowing where God would lead:

   By faith Abraham, when he was called to go out into a place which he should after receive for an inheritance, obeyed; *and he went out, not knowing whither he went.* By faith he sojourned in the land of promise, as in a strange country, dwelling in tabernacles with Isaac, and Jacob, the heirs with him of the same promise (Hebrews 11:8-9).

   Later in his life, he was willing to offer his only son:

   By faith Abraham, when he was tried, offered up Isaac: and he that received the promises offered up his only begotten son, Of whom it is said, That in Isaac shall thy seed be called: Accounting that God was able to raise him up, even from the dead; from whence also he received him in a figure (Hebrews 11:17-19).

5. *Noah's faith was characterized by fear and hard work.*
By faith Noah, being warned of God of things not seen as yet, *moved with fear, prepared an ark to the saving of his house;* by the which he condemned the world, and became heir of the righteousness which is by faith (Hebrews 11:7).

It took Noah 120 years to build that ark!

6. *The faith of Moses was characterized by his willingness to forsake the world.*
By faith Moses, when he was born, was hid three months of his parents, because they saw he was a proper child; and they were afraid of the king's commandment. By faith Moses, when he was come to years, *refused to be called the son of Pharaoh's daughter; Choosing rather to suffer affliction with the people of God, than to enjoy the pleasures of sin for a season* (Hebrews 11:23-25).

7. *Sometimes faith is characterized by a willingness to suffer greatly.*
...and others were tortured, not accepting deliverance; that they might obtain a better resurrection: And others had trial of cruel mocking and scourging, yea, moreover of bonds and imprisonment: They were stoned, they were sawn asunder, were tempted, were slain with the sword: they wandered about in sheepskins and goatskins; being destitute, afflicted, tormented; (Of whom the world was not worthy;) they wandered in deserts, and in mountains, and in dens and caves of the earth (Hebrews 11:35b-38).

8. *Faith is the basis of a believer's life.*
Behold, his soul which is lifted up is not upright in him: *but the just shall live by his faith* (Habakkuk 2:4).

9. *By faith God provides for a believer's needs.*
And why take ye thought for raiment? Consider the lilies of the field, how they grow; they toil not, neither do they spin: And yet I say unto you, That even Solomon in all his glory was not arrayed like one of these. Wherefore, if God so clothe the grass of the field, which today is, and tomorrow is cast into the oven, *shall He not more clothe you, O ye of little faith* (Matthew 6:28-30)?

10. *Faith has a sanctifying effect in hearts.*
And God, which knoweth the hearts, bare them witness, giving them the Holy Ghost, even as he did unto us; and put no difference between us and them, *purifying their hearts by faith* (Acts 15:8-9).

11. *Faith is involved in propitiation.*
Whom God hath set forth to be a propitiation through faith in His blood, to declare His righteousness for the remission of sins that are past, through the forbearance of God; To declare, I say, at this time His righteousness (Romans 3:25-26a).

12. Strong faith glorifies God.
He staggered not at the promise of God through unbelief; *but was strong in faith, giving glory to God;* And being fully persuaded that, what He had promised, He was able also to perform (Romans 4:20-21).

13. Justification is based on faith.
Therefore being justified by faith, we have peace with God through our Lord Jesus Christ (Romans 5:1).

14. Hearing the Word of God produces faith.
So then faith cometh by hearing, and hearing by the Word of God (Romans 10:17).

15. Faith is eternal.
And now abideth faith, hope, charity, these three... (I Corinthians 13:13).

16. Faith looks forward to better things from God.
Therefore we are always confident, knowing that, whilst we are at home in the body, we are absent from the Lord; (For we walk by faith, not by sight:) *We are confident, I say, and willing rather to be absent from the body, and to be present with the Lord* (II Corinthians 5:6-8).

17. Faith is a fruit of the Spirit which grows in a believer's life.
But the fruit of the Spirit is love, joy, peace, longsuffering, gentleness, goodness, faith (Galatians 5:22).

18. Faith is absolutely essential to salvation.
For by grace are ye saved through faith; and that not of yourselves: it is the gift of God (Ephesians 2:8).

19. Faith is a very important part of the armor that God provides.
In one passage it is described as a breastplate:
But let us, who are of the day, be sober, *putting on the breastplate of faith* and love... (I Thessalonians 5:8).

In another passage it is described as a shield:
Above all, *taking the shield of faith,* wherewith ye shall be able to quench all the fiery darts of the wicked (Ephesians 6:16).

20. Faith involves sacrifice.
Yea, and if I be offered upon the sacrifice and service of your faith, I joy, and rejoice with you all (Philippians 2:17).

21. A faithful ministry can help perfect the faith of others.
For what thanks can we render to God again for you, for all the joy wherewith

we joy for your sakes before our God; Night and day praying exceedingly that we might see your face, *and might perfect that which is lacking in your faith* (I Thessalonians 9-10)?

22. Faith is closely connected with patience.
So that we ourselves glory in you in the churches of God for your patience and *faith in all your persecutions and tribulations that ye endure* (II Thessalonians 1:4).

Knowing this, *that the trying of your faith worketh patience* (James 1:3).

23. It is important that faith be genuine.
I thank God, Whom I serve from my forefathers with pure conscience, that without ceasing I have remembrance of thee in my prayers night and day; Greatly desiring to see thee, being mindful of thy tears, that I may be filled with joy; When I call to remembrance *the unfeigned faith that is in thee...*(II Timothy 1:3-5a).

24. Our approach to God in prayer should be in faith.
Having therefore, brethren, boldness to enter the holiest by the blood of Jesus, By a new and living way, which He hath consecrated for us, through the veil, that is to say, His flesh: And having an high priest over the house of God: *Let us draw nigh with a true heart in full assurance of faith,* having our hearts sprinkled from an evil conscience... (Hebrews 10:19-22a).

25. Jesus is the Author and Finisher of our faith.
Looking unto Jesus, *the author and finisher of our faith;* Who for the joy that was set before Him endured the cross. Despising the shame, and is set down at the right hand of the throne of God (Hebrews 12:2).

26. Real faith produces good works.
Even so *faith, if it hath not works, is dead, being alone* (James 2:17).

A simple way to explain the relationship between faith and good works would go something like this: a man is not saved by doing good works, but he will do good works if he is saved!

27. We should defend our faith vigorously.
Beloved, when I gave all diligence to write unto you of the common salvation, it was needful for me to write unto you, and exhort you that ye should *earnestly contend for the faith which was once delivered unto the saints* (Jude 3).

But sanctify the Lord God in your hearts: and *be ready always to give an answer to every man that asketh you a reason of the hope that is in you* with meekness and fear (I Peter 3:15).

Surely we would do well if we could say with the Apostle Paul,

I have fought a good fight, I have finished my course, *I have kept the faith* (II Timothy 4:7).

My Faith Looks up to Thee
Ray Palmer

My faith looks up to Thee,
Thou Lamb of Calvary,
Savior divine;
Now hear me when I pray,
Take all my sin away;
O let me from this day
Be wholly Thine!

May Thy rich grace impart
Strength to my fainting heart,
My zeal inspire:
As Thou hast died for me,
O may my love to Thee
Pure, warm, and changeless be—
A living fire!

XXXI

Repentance

Now after that John was put in prison, Jesus came into Galilee, preaching the Gospel of the kingdom of God, And saying, The time is fulfilled, and the kingdom of God is at hand: repent ye, and believe the Gospel (Mark 1:14-15).

It seems that strong preaching and teaching against sin is not well received in many churches today. Somehow it just isn't "politically correct" to make people feel uncomfortable, especially when it comes to spiritual matters.

This, of course, has been a problem that ministers of the Gospel have had to deal with ever since our Lord came to this earth and died for man's sin.

To be faithful to what our Lord proclaimed and what the Scriptures teach, however, repentance is an important truth that *must* be proclaimed.

Faith is positive because it trusts. Repentance is negative because it repudiates a past life that was full of sin and unbelief.

The Greek verb "to repent" is *metanoeo*. As was pointed out earlier in this book, it means "to change one's mind." In our natural, unsaved state we sin constantly and think little or nothing about it. As long as we can "get by" with that sin, we have no fear of consequences from either man or God.

When the truth of God's Word and the conviction of the Holy Spirit become realities, repentance is the proper response to our realization of sin and its awful consequences.

Perhaps this illustration will help. Imagine you are driving rapidly toward a cliff, not realizing that it lies just ahead until it is almost too late. Then someone alerts you to the fact that you must turn around quickly or face certain death!

One who refuses to repent will ignore such a warning and soon will crash and die.

One who *does* repent will slam on his brakes very quickly, turn the vehicle around without delay, and determine *never* to do anything so dangerous again!

It is the use of the brakes, the turning around of the vehicle, and the decision to avoid anything that poses such danger that correctly illustrates repentance.

Genuine repentance will take quick action to deal completely with sin: to stop doing it, to start living for God, and to determine that going back to the "old ways" is *not* an option!

Just as faith had intellectual, emotional, and volitional elements, so does genuine repentance.

1. *Intellectual.*
The actual meaning of the verb "to repent" is "to change one's mind."
Therefore by the deeds of the Law there shall no flesh be justified in His sight: *for by the Law is the knowledge of sin* (Romans 3:20).

Who *knowing the judgment of God,* that they which commit such things are worthy of death, not only do the same, but have pleasure in them that do them (Romans 1:32).

For I acknowledge my transgressions: and my sin is ever before me (Psalm 51:3).

2. *Emotional.*
Sometimes repentance brings tears; other times it brings the uneasiness of conviction of sin; sometimes the emotion of repentance brings both feelings.
Have mercy upon me, O God, according to Thy lovingkindness: according unto the multitude of Thy tender mercies blot out my transgressions (Psalm 51:1).

Now I rejoice, not that ye were made sorry, but that ye sorrowed to repentance: For ye were made sorry after a godly manner, that ye might receive damage by us in nothing. For godly sorrow worketh repentance to salvation not to be repented of: but the sorrow of the world worketh death. For behold this selfsame thing, that ye *sorrowed* after a godly sort, what carefulness it wrought in you, yea, what clearing of yourselves, yea, what indignation, yea, what fear, yea, what vehement desire, yea, what zeal, yea, what revenge! In all things ye have approved yourselves to be clear in this matter (II Corinthians 7:9-11).

Verse 10 here is especially important. "Godly sorrow worketh repentance to salvation" and the "sorrow of the world worketh death." Godly sorrow has the other elements of repentance in it. The sorrow of the world described here is strong emotion that lasts for only a short time. In the realm of spiritual matters, such shallow emotion is not only worthless, it is actually very harmful because "it worketh death."

3. *Volitional.*
This aspect of repentance involves the determination to avoid sin and to follow God with His help.
Create in me a clean heart, O God; and renew a right heart within me (Psalm 51:10).

Consider the case of Zacchaeus, a wealthy tax collector who realized his sin and came to Christ with urgency:

And Zacchaeus stood, and said unto the Lord; Behold, Lord, the half of my goods I give to the poor; *and if I have taken any thing from any man by false accusation, I restore him fourfold.* And Jesus said unto him, This day is salvation come to this house, forasmuch as he also is a son of Abraham. For the Son of man is come to seek and save that which was lost (Luke 18:8-10).

Below are other Scriptures that shed light on repentance and its importance:

1. *It is essential to salvation.*

There were present at that season some that told Him of the Galileans, whose blood Pilate had mingled with their sacrifices. And Jesus answering said unto them, Suppose ye that these Galileans were sinners above all Galileans, because they suffered such things? I tell you, Nay: *but except ye repent, ye shall all likewise perish.* Or those eighteen, upon whom the tower in Siloam fell, and slew them, think ye that they were sinners above all men that dwell in Jerusalem? I tell you, Nay: *but except ye repent, ye shall all likewise perish* (Luke 13:1-5).

Paul stressed the importance of repentance when he talked with king Agrippa:

Whereupon, O king Agrippa, I was not disobedient unto the heavenly vision: But showed first unto them of Damascus, and at Jerusalem, and throughout all the coasts of Judaea, and then to the Gentiles, *that they should repent and turn to God,* and do works meet for repentance (Acts 26:19-20).

2. *It is equivalent to faith.*

Paul made this point in his last contact with the Ephesian elders:
Testifying both to the Jews, and also to the Greeks, *repentance toward God, and faith toward our Lord Jesus Christ* (Acts 20:21).

The equivalence of repentance and faith is clear in the wording of the Greek original. The word "repentance" has a definite article before it; then comes the word "and;" then comes the word "faith" without the definite article. When this grammatical construction appears in Greek the two words are equivalent.

One might well think of repentance and faith as two sides of the same coin!

3. *Repentance precedes baptism.*

Then Peter said unto them, *Repent,* and be baptized every one of you in the name of Jesus Christ (Acts 2:38a).

4. *Repentance is for sinners, not "righteous people."*

But when Jesus heard that, He said unto them, They that be whole need not a physician, but they that are sick. But go ye and learn what that meaneth, I will have mercy, and not sacrifice: *for I am not come to call the righteous, but sinners to repentance* (Matthew 9:12-13).

5. **God is the source of repentance.**
Or despisest thou the riches of His goodness and forbearance and longsuffering: not knowing that *the goodness of God leadeth thee to repentance* (Romans 2:4)?

6. **God wants all to repent and be saved.**
The Lord is not slack concerning His promise, as some men count slackness; but is longsuffering to us-ward, *not willing that any should perish, but that all should come to repentance* (II Peter 3:9).

7. **Even in Old Testament times God's people understood that true repentance involved a determination to forsake sin.**
Surely it is meet to be said unto God, I have borne chastisement, *I will not offend any more* (Job 34:31).

8. **Healing comes after repentance.**
He healeth the broken in heart, and bindeth up their wounds (Psalm 147:3).

Out of my bondage, sorrow, and night,
Jesus, I come, Jesus I come;
Into Thy freedom, gladness, and light,
Jesus, I come to Thee!
Out of my sickness, into Thy health;
Out of my sin and into Thyself,
Jesus, I come to Thee!

Out of unrest and arrogant pride,
Jesus, I come, Jesus I come;
Into Thy blessed will to abide,
Jesus, I come to Thee;
Out of myself to dwell in Thy love,
Out of despair into raptures above;
Upward for aye on wings like a dove,
Jesus, I come to Thee!

Jesus, I Come
William T. Sleeper

XXXII

The Blood of Christ

And almost all things are by the Law purged with blood; and without shedding of blood is no remission (Hebrews 9:22).

God has been revealing the importance of blood sacrifices since the time of Adam and Eve. After they fell into sin, God realized they had a need for clothing and some hope for forgiveness.

Unto Adam and to his wife did the Lord God make coats of skins, and clothed them (Genesis 3:21).

The word "blood" does not appear here, but the implication is that God killed an animal, and therefore its blood was shed. The Lamb of God died thousands of years later, providing a way for mankind to be saved, allowing righteousness to be imputed from Him to those who believe. The coats of skin are pictures of "putting on the new man" (Colossians 3:9-10). Thus we see that this act in Genesis was a picture of what Jesus did for Christians.

Did Adam and Eve understand that Jesus was their Savior? Of course, the answer is "no," but they did understand that God was both holy and loving and that blood was shed so that they would not be ashamed.

There is a steady revelation about the blood throughout the Old Testament. The same can be said for grace and faith. These three bedrock truths have been an important part of God's revelation to man since the very beginning.

Below is a partial listing of the Old Testament's teaching about the blood:

1. ***Abel's sacrifice was acceptable to God because an animal was offered, and therefore blood was shed.***
   And in the process of time it came to pass, That Cain brought of the fruit of the ground an offering unto the Lord, And Abel, *he also brought of the firstlings of his flock and of the fat thereof.* And the Lord had respect unto Abel and to his offering: but unto Cain and his offering he had not respect. And Cain was very wroth, and his countenance fell (Genesis 4:3-5).

   The rest of this story is revealed in verses 6-16 of this chapter. We can see what happens when somebody tries to change God's standard into something else, even though there was some effort made to make an offering to God.

   Cain undoubtedly worked hard to produce "the fruit of the ground" which he offered to God. He probably felt that his offering was just as good as Abel's, but when Cain made the decision to ignore God's directions regarding sacrifices, to become rebellious in not making the adjustment to offer what God insisted on, and to kill his brother Abel, he fell very deep into sin and paid a heavy price as a result:

And Cain said unto the Lord, *My punishment is greater than I can bear* (Genesis 4:13).

This story illustrates how important it is to follow God's directions! Religions today have come up with substitute ways to appear "good," but in the end they are not recognizing that God has provided only one way to be saved, and the consequences of not believing Him are very heavy indeed, just as they were for Cain.

2. ***God revealed even more about the blood when He gave instructions to Moses about the Passover.***
Your lamb shall be without blemish, a male of the first year: ye shall take it out from the sheep, or from the goats: And ye shall keep it up until the fourteenth day of the same month... (Exodus 12:6a).

And they shall take of the blood, and strike it on the two sideposts and on the upper door post of the houses, wherein they shall eat it. And they shall eat the flesh that night, roast with fire, and unleavened bread: and with bitter herbs they shall eat it. *And the blood shall be to you for a token upon the houses where ye are:* and when I see the blood, I will pass over you (Exodus 12:7-8,13a).

These verses instruct that the lamb be "without spot," just as Jesus was sinless; and the blood was to be smeared clearly on the entrance to the house, just as believers are to have the blood of Christ applied to their hearts.

The results? When the Father sees the blood applied, deliverance is immediate, and the consequences of ignoring or disobeying God's command is death (Exodus 12:29).

3. ***Blood was a part of many of the offerings prescribed by God soon after the first Passover.***
The following offerings required blood: the sin offerings (Leviticus 4:5-17), burnt offering (Exodus 29:16), atonement (Leviticus 16:14-18), trespass (Leviticus 7:2), peace (Leviticus 3:2-13), and the blood of the covenant (Exodus 24:5-8).

4. ***God revealed clearly that both life and atonement for sin are in the blood.***
For the *life* of the flesh is in the blood: and I have given it to you upon the altar *to make an atonement for your souls: for it is the blood that maketh atonement for the soul* (Leviticus 17:11).

The "trail of blood" continues throughout the Old Testament. Surely Isaiah understood the importance of the blood when he wrote Isaiah 53; and so did David when he wrote Psalm 22.

Below is a list of the New Testament's teaching on the blood of Christ:

1. *At the last supper, the Lord instructed that the cup was representative of His shed blood.*
   And He took the cup, and gave thanks, and gave it to them, saying, Drink ye all of it; *For this is My blood of the New Testament,* which is shed for many for the remission of sins (Matthew 26:28).

2. *The crown of thorns upon His head, the nails in His hands and feet, the scourging before the crucifixion, and the piercing of His side with a spear produced the blood, that sinless blood, which redeemed us from our sins!*
   Read John 19.

3. *The church universal was purchased by Christ's blood.*
   In his farewell meeting with the Ephesian elders, Paul said,

   Take heed, to *feed the church of God, which He hath purchased with His own blood* (Acts 20:28).

4. *Christ's blood is the basis for propitiation.*
   Whom God hath set forth to be a propitiation through faith in His blood, to declare His righteousness for the remission of sins that are past (Romans 3:25a).

5. *Christ's blood is the basis of justification.*
   Much more then, *being now justified by His blood,* we shall be saved from wrath through Him (Romans 5:9).

6. *Christ's blood is the basis of reconciliation.*
   And that He might reconcile both unto God in one body by the cross, having slain the enmity thereby (Ephesians 2:16).

   But now in Christ Jesus ye who sometimes were far off *are made nigh by the blood of Christ.* For He is our peace, Who hath made us both one, and hath broken down the middle wall of partition between us; Having abolished in His flesh the enmity... (Ephesians 2:13-15a).

7. *Christ's blood is the basis for forgiveness, both in salvation and fellowship.*
   In Whom we have *redemption through His blood, the forgiveness of sins,* according to the riches of His grace: Wherein He hath abounded toward us in all wisdom and prudence (Ephesians 1:7-8).

If we walk in the light as He is in the light, *we have fellowship one with another, and the blood of Jesus Christ His Son cleanseth us from all sin* (I John 1:7).

8. *Christ's blood is vastly superior to the blood of bulls and goats.*
But Christ being come an high priest of good things to come, by a greater and more perfect tabernacle, not made with hands, that is to say, not of this building; *Neither by the blood of goats and calves, but by His own blood* He entered in once into the holy place, having obtained eternal redemption for us (Hebrews 9:11-12).

9. *Christ's blood has great sanctifying power.*
Wherefore Jesus also, *that He might sanctify the people with His own blood,* suffered without the gate (Hebrews 13:12).

10. *Christ's blood is the basis for the everlasting covenant.*
Now the God of peace, that brought again from the dead our Lord Jesus, that great Shepherd of the sheep, *through the blood of the everlasting covenant* (Hebrews 13:20).

11. *Christ's blood is the means to overcome Satan.*
And the great dragon was cast out, that old serpent, called the Devil, and Satan, which deceiveth the whole world; he was cast out into the earth, and his angels were cast out with him. And I heard a loud voice saying in heaven, Now is come salvation, and strength, and the kingdom of our God, and the power of His Christ: for the accuser of the brethren is cast down, which accused them before our God day and night. *And they overcame him by the blood of the Lamb,* and by the word of their testimony; and they loved not their lives unto the death (Revelation 12:9-11).

Christ our Redeemer died on the cross,
Died for the sinner,
Paid all his due;
Sprinkle your soul in the blood of the Lamb,
And I will pass, will pass over you!

O great compassion! O boundless love!
O lovingkindness,
Faithful and true!
Find peace and shelter under the blood,
And I will pass, will pass over you!

When I See the Blood
John Foote

XXXIII

Christ's Resurrection

The former treatise have I made, O Theophilus, of all that Jesus began both to do and teach, until the day in which He was taken up, after that He through the Holy Ghost had given commandments unto the Apostles whom He had chosen: To whom He showed Himself alive...by many infallible proofs...(Acts 1:1-3a).

One of the most interesting studies in the Scriptures is the reaction of the disciples between the time of our Lord's death on the cross and their realization that He had risen from the grave.

In the first place, they had ample evidence from the Old Testament that God does on occasion raise people from the dead:

1. *Job believed in life after death.*
   O that Thou wouldest hide me in the grave, that Thou wouldest keep me in secret, until Thy wrath be past, that Thou wouldest appoint me a set time, and remember me! *If a man die, shall he live again? All the days of my appointed time will I wait, till my change come* (Job 14:13-14).

   For I know that my Redeemer liveth, and that He shall stand at the latter day upon the earth: And though after my skin worms destroy this body, *yet in my flesh I shall see God: Whom I shall see for myself,* and mine eyes shall behold, and not another; though my reins be consumed within me (Job 19:25-27).

2. *David also believed in life after death.*
   Therefore my heart is glad, and my glory rejoiceth: *my flesh also shall rest in hope. For Thou wilt not leave my soul in hell:* neither wilt Thou suffer Thine Holy One to see corruption. Thou wilt show me the path of life... (Psalm 16:9-10).

3. *There were resurrections in Old Testament times.*
   God allowed Elijah to raise up the widow's son (I Kings 17:9-24); God allowed Elisha to raise up the Shanammite's son (II Kings 4:32-36); and while a dead man was being buried, his body touched the bones of Elisha and he was revived (II Kings 13:21).

4. *Abraham fully expected to return with his son Isaac after offering him as a sacrifice.*
   And Abraham said unto his young men, Abide ye here with the ass and I and the lad will go yonder and worship, *and come again to you* (Genesis 22:5).

   Later, of course, God provided a ram as a sacrifice (Genesis 22:13).

5. **Isaiah wrote about a resurrection.**

We have been with child, we have been in pain, we have as it were brought forth wind; we have not wrought any deliverance in the earth; neither have the inhabitants of the world fallen. *Thy dead men shall live, together with my dead body shall they arise.* Awake and sing, ye that dwell in the dust: for thy dew is as the dew of herbs, and the earth shall cast out the dead (Isaiah 26:19).

6. **Hosea also wrote about a resurrection.**

I will ransom them from the power of the grave; I will redeem them from death: O death, I will be thy plagues; O grave, I will be thy destruction: repentance shall be his from mine eyes (Hosea 13:14).

In addition to all this evidence from the Old Testament, consider all the evidence Jesus had presented to them:

1. **He raised three people from the dead during His ministry.**

The son of a widow from Nain.

And when the Lord saw her, He had compassion on her, and said unto her, Weep not. And He came and touched the bier: and they that bare him stood still. And He said, *Young man, I say unto thee, Arise. And he that was dead began to speak* (Luke 7:13-15a).

Jairus' daughter.

And when Jesus came into the ruler's house, and saw the minstrels and the people making a noise, He said unto them, Give place: for the maid is not dead, but sleepeth. And they laughed Him to scorn. But when the people were put forth, He went in, and took her by the hand, *and the maid arose* (Matthew 9:23-25).

Lazarus.

And when He had spoken, He cried with a loud voice, Lazarus, come forth. *And he that was dead came forth,* bound hand and foot with graveclothes: and his face was bound about with a napkin. Jesus saith unto them, Loose him, and let him go. Then many of the Jews which came to Mary, and had seen the things which did, believed on Him (John 11:43-45).

2. **Jesus had prophesied about the future resurrection of believers.**

Verily, verily, I say unto you, The hour is coming, and now is, *when the dead shall hear the voice of the Son of God; and they that hear shall live.* For as the Father hath life in Himself; so hath He given to the Son to have life in Himself; Marvel not at this: for the hour is coming, in the which all that are in the graves shall hear His voice, *And they shall come forth* (John 5:25-26, 28-29a).

For I came down from heaven, not to do Mine own will, but the will of Him that sent Me. And this is the Father's will which sent Me. That of all which He hath given Me I should lose nothing, but should raise it up again at the last day. And this is the will of Him that sent Me, that every one which seeth the Son, and believeth on Him, may have everlasting life: and *I will raise him up at the last day* (John 6:38-40).

And thou shalt be blessed: for they cannot recompense thee, for *thou shalt to recompensed at the resurrection of the just* (Luke 14:14).

And Jesus answering said unto them, The children of this world marry, and are given in marriage: but they which shall be accounted worthy to obtain that world, *and the resurrection from the dead,* neither marry, nor are given in marriage: Neither can they die any more (Luke 20:34-36a).

3. ***Jesus told His disciples of His own resurrection.***
But He answered and said unto them, An evil and adulterous generation seeketh after a sign; and there shall no sign be given to it, but the sign of the prophet Jonas: For *as Jonas was three days and three nights in the whale's belly; so shall the Son of man be three days and three nights in the heart of the earth* (Matthew 12:39-40).

From that time forth began Jesus to show unto His disciples, how He must go unto Jerusalem, and suffer many things of the elders and chief priests and scribes, and be killed, *and be raised again the third day* (Matthew 16:21; also Mark 8:31).

And Jesus going up to Jerusalem took the twelve disciples apart in the way, and said unto them, Behold, we go up to Jerusalem: and the Son of man shall be betrayed unto the chief priests and unto the scribes, and they shall condemn Him to death, And shall deliver Him to the Gentiles to mock and to scourge, and to crucify Him: *and the third day He shall rise again* (Matthew 20:17-19).

For He taught His disciples, and said unto them, The Son of man is delivered into the hands of men, and they shall kill Him; and after that He is killed, *He shall rise the third day.* But they understood not that saying, and were afraid to ask Him (Mark 9:31-32).

Therefore doth My Father love Me, because I lay down My life. *That I might take it again.* No man taketh it from Me, but I lay it down of Myself. I have power to lay it down, *and I have power to take it again.* This commandment have I received of My Father. There was a division therefore among the Jews for these sayings (John 10:17-18).

Even after our Lord died and rose, there was still a time of doubt.

Then the eleven disciples went away in Galilee, into a mountain where Jesus had appointed them. And when they saw Him, they worshipped Him: *but some doubted* (Matthew 28:16-17).

It was Mary Magdalene, and Joanna, and Mary the mother of James, and other women that were with them, which told these things unto the Apostles. *And their words seemed to them as idle tales, and they believed them not* (Luke 24:10-11).

But Thomas, one of the twelve, called Didymus, was not with them when Jesus came. The other disciples therefore said unto him, We have seen the Lord. But he said unto them, Except I shall see in His hands the print of the nails, and put my finger into the print of the nails, and thrust my hand into His side, *I will not believe* (John 20:24-25).

Our Lord said some mildly rebuking words to the two Emmaus disciples:

Then He said unto them, *O fools, and slow of heart to believe* all that the prophets have spoken: Ought not Christ to have suffered these things, and to enter into His glory (Luke 24:25-26)?

It was not until God did a special work in their hearts and minds that they finally believed:

And He said unto them, These are the words which I have spoken unto you, while I was yet with you, that all things must be fulfilled, which were written in the law of Moses, and the prophets, and in the psalms, concerning Me. *Then opened He their understanding, that they might understand the Scriptures,* And said unto them, Thus it is written, and thus it behooved Christ to suffer, *and to rise from the dead the third day* (Luke 24:44-46).

Surely the resurrection of Jesus Christ is the greatest event in all of history!

Once the disciples realized our Lord was risen, they spent the rest of their lives preaching, living, and defending the resurrection. They also gave their very lives for their faith in a risen Savior!

There are four considerations to be made about the resurrection:

1.   *Its nature.*
There are some who try to suggest that Jesus did not actually die but somehow survived and wandered off into obscurity. This, of course, is not supported by any evidence.

The centurion and soldiers declared that Jesus had died (Mark 15:45; John 19:33); the women who came to the tomb were there to anoint the dead body of our Savior (Mark 16:1); *water and blood* flowed from His side (John 19:34); and the disciples were greatly surprised and thrilled to know He was not dead but risen again (Matthew 28:17; Luke 24:37f; John 20:3-9).

The resurrection of Jesus Christ was *bodily.*

Jesus declared after His resurrection that He had flesh and bones (Luke 24:39); He was recognized by His own after it happened (John 20:25-28); He ate food after He arose (Luke 24:41-43); and the angels at the tomb said He had risen "as He had said" (Luke 24:6-8).

The resurrection of Jesus Christ was *unique.*

Others who had been resurrected (Old and New Testaments) undoubtedly died again, but Jesus still lives (Romans 6:9f).

In addition, He was able to pass through closed doors (John 20:19).

2. ***Its importance.***
    The resurrection of Jesus Christ is mentioned in every sermon in the book of Acts, and Paul emphasizes the significance of His resurrection, especially in I Corinthians 15.

Our preaching and faith are empty if He is not risen.
And if Christ be not risen, *then is our preaching vain, and your faith is also vain* (I Corinthians 15:14).

What would be the point of preaching something or believing something that is not true?

If the Apostles are false witnesses about the resurrection, how can their testimony about anything else be trusted? And if their testimony is not to be trusted, how can anyone truly believe in the Gospel or any message in the Bible?

Yea, *and we are found false witnesses of God;* because we have testified of God that He raised up Christ: Whom He raised not up, if so be that the dead rise not (I Corinthians 15:15).

Salvation cannot be a reality without His resurrection.
And if Christ be not raised, *your faith is vain; ye are yet in your sins* (I Corinthians 15:17).

How could a dead Savior offer eternal life? How could a Savior be trusted if He prophesied His own resurrection but is still in the grave?

Those who died but had trusted in Christ have simply perished if Christ did not rise from the grave.
Then they also which are fallen asleep in Christ are perished (I Corinthians 15:18).

They simply would have followed "another religious leader" who made great claims but could not back them up!

The whole idea of Christianity is worthless if He is not risen!
If in this life only we have hope in Christ, *we are of all men most miserable* (I Corinthians 15:19).

Why follow something fervently when it is all a hoax? Only miserable or deluded people do something like that!

3. *The evidence for it.*
He made twelve recorded post-resurrection appearances.
He appeared to Mary (Mark 16:9; John 20:11-18), to other women (Matthew 28: 9f), to the Emmaus disciples (Mark 16:12f; Luke 24:13-33), to Peter (Luke 24:34; I Corinthians 15:5), to ten of the Apostles (John 20:19-24), to eleven of the Apostles, including Thomas (John 20:26-29), to more than five hundred at the same time (I Corinthians 15:6), to James (I Corinthians 15:7), to the Apostles just before His ascension (Mark 16:9; Luke 24:50f; Acts 1:9), and to Paul (Acts 15:8).

He was touched after the resurrection.
Concerning Mary and Mary Magdalene, Matthew records the following:

And as they went to tell His disciples, behold, Jesus met them, saying, All hail. And they *came and held Him by the feet,* and worshipped Him (Matthew 28:9).

Mary met the Lord and touched Him (recorded by John):

Jesus saith unto her, Mary. She turned herself, and saith unto Him, Rabboni; which is to say, Master. Jesus saith unto her, *Touch Me not;* for I am not yet ascended to My Father , and your Father; and to my God, and your God. Mary Magdalene came and told the disciples that she had seen the Lord, and that He had spoken these things unto her (John 20:16-18).

"Touch Me not" is a present tense imperative in the Greek, clearly indicating that she was touching Him but needed to stop it. A better translation would be, "Stop touching Me."

Two passages indicate that the grave clothes were left in the grave and yet wrapped neatly:

Then arose Peter, and ran unto the sepulcher; and stooping down, *he beheld the linen clothes laid by themselves*, and departed, wondering in himself at that which was come to pass (Luke 24:12; see also John 20:3-8).

These two passages are very significant. If Christ's body had been stolen, those who took it would have had to overpower the Roman guards, break the seal of the Roman government that was placed in front of the tomb, roll a very large stone away, and take off the grave clothes, *leaving those grave clothes wrapped neatly in a place by itself!*

What grave robber is going to take the time to neatly arrange the linen!?

On the other hand, when Christ arose, He rose triumphantly, and He took the time to leave such convincing evidence behind. Why would He be in such a hurry? He is the Son of God, and He wanted all who will look honestly at the evidence to realize that He really did rise from that grave!

Even doubting Thomas was convinced of His resurrection.

Then came Jesus, the doors being shut, and stood in the midst, and said, Peace be unto you. Then saith He to Thomas, Reach hither thy finger, and behold My hands; and reach hither thy hand, and thrust it into My side: and be not faithless, but believing. And Thomas answered and said unto Him, My Lord and my God! Jesus saith unto him, *Thomas, because thou hast seen Me, thou hast believed:* blessed are they that have not seen, and yet have believed. And many other signs truly did Jesus in the presence of His disciples, which are not written in this book (John 20:26-30).

4. *Results of His resurrection.*
It shows He really is God. All of the religions of the world have a founder whose body is still in a grave somewhere, but our Lord is alive!
And declared to be the Son of God with power, according to the Spirit of holiness, by the resurrection from the dead (Romans 1:4).

He can legitimately provide justification for those who believe.
But for us also, to whom it shall be imputed, if we believe on Him that raised up Jesus our Lord from the dead; *Who was delivered for our offenses, and was raised again for our justification* (Romans 4:24-25).

He is able to intercede for those who believe.
Who is he that condemneth? It is Christ that died, yea rather, that is risen again, *Who is even at the right hand of God, Who also maketh intercession for us* (Romans 8:34).

He was able to send the Holy Spirit to believers.

This Jesus hath God raised up, whereof we all are witnesses. Therefore being by the right hand of God exalted, *and having received of the Father the promise of the Holy Ghost, He hath sent forth this,* which ye now see and hear (Acts 2:32-33).

He is able to empower believers in many ways.
The eyes of your understanding being enlightened; that ye may know what is the hope of His calling, and what is the riches of the glory of His inheritance in the saints, *And what is the exceeding greatness of His power to us-ward who believe, according to the working of His mighty power, Which He wrought in Christ, when He raised Him from the dead,* and set Him at His own right hand in the heavenly places (Ephesians 1:18-20).

He is able to promise a resurrection for believers.
But if the Spirit of Him that raised up Jesus from the dead dwell in you, *He that raised up Christ from the dead shall also quicken your mortal bodies by the Spirit that dwelleth in you* (Romans 8:11).

He will judge all men righteously.
Because He hath appointed a day, in the which *He will judge the world in righteousness by that man whom He hath ordained; whereof He hath given assurance to all men, in that He hath raised Him from the dead* (Acts 17:32).

Low in the grave He lay—
Jesus, my Savior!
Waiting the coming day—
Jesus, my Lord!

Death cannot keep his prey—
Jesus, my Savior!
He tore the bars away—
Jesus, my Lord!

Up from the grave He arose,
With a mighty triumph o'er His foes!
He arose a victor from the dark domain,
And He lives forever with His saints to reign!
He arose! He arose!
Hallelujah! Christ arose!

Christ Arose
Robert Lowry

Section IV: The Practicality of Our Salvation
Concluding Thoughts

. . . and ye shall be witnesses. . . (Acts 1:8).

This conclusion includes a chapter on encouragement for believers and an invitation for unbelievers.

XXXIV

Encouragement for Believers

And my soul shall be joyful in the Lord: it shall rejoice in His salvation
(Psalm 35:9).

Can anyone doubt that God has provided a complete salvation? From eternity past to eternity future He has met the needs of His beloved. He has demonstrated His wisdom, holiness, immutability, and amazing love!

What should be our response? Obviously, we should (and will) praise Him forever!

In addition, Christians should take courage while serving the Lord in this life. It is the purpose of this chapter to give believers reasons to ponder God's goodness in providing such a wonderful salvation.

God gives us richly "all things to enjoy" (I Timothy 6:17).

Below is a list of great truths that believers should ponder and enjoy:

1. Do you ever feel neglected?
    God foreknew, chose, and predestinated your salvation before creation!

2. Do you ever feel worthless?
    You have been made a new creature by regeneration!

3. Do you ever feel enslaved or trapped?
    You have been redeemed and set free by His blood!

4. Do you ever feel your sin hasn't been paid for?
    You have a holy standing before God in positional sanctification!

5. Do you ever feel that Satan is winning battles in your spiritual life?
    God has actually declared you not only "not guilty," but "absolutely righteous" in justification! Satan cannot overturn such a declaration!

6. Do you ever feel that you don't belong to God?
    You have been Spirit baptized into His body and adopted into His family!

7. Do you ever feel you have no place in God's work?
    He has made you an ambassador and a priest!

8. Do you ever feel helpless to learn or make good decisions?
    The Holy Spirit indwells you!

9. Do you ever feel you need power or boldness to serve the Lord? How about needing help in your relationships?
   The Holy Spirit fills believers who totally surrender to Him!

10. Do you ever feel you don't have the ability to serve the Lord?
    He has given all of us spiritual gifts!

11. Do you ever feel you lack the grace to serve others?
    He has given you the fruit of the Spirit!

12. Do you ever feel God is angry at you?
    The blood of Christ has propitiated that anger!

13. Do you ever feel you are not close to God?
    You have been reconciled to God!

14. Do you ever feel your sin is so horrible that God will always hold it against you?
    Your sins are forgiven and forgotten!

15. Do you ever feel Satan might steal your salvation?
    God has sealed your salvation and has made promises about it which He cannot break!

16. Do you ever feel that you have no right to be happy in this life?
    God has provided you with liberty!

17. Do you ever feel that you cannot win when temptation comes?
    God has provided you with all the armor you need!

18. Do you ever feel that life isn't really all that exciting?
    You have ultimate sanctification and glorification in heaven forever!

19. Do you ever feel you don't get what you deserve?
    You will receive rewards in heaven for faithfulness!

20. Do you ever feel powerless to make a difference?
    You will reign with Christ!

After looking at such a list as this, surely we can agree with the Apostle Paul, who said,

He that spared not His own Son, but delivered Him up for us all, *how shall He not with Him freely give us all things? Who shall lay any thing to the charge of God's elect* (Romans 8:32-33a)?

The cross, it standeth fast,
Hallelujah! Hallelujah!
Defying every blast,
Hallelujah! Hallelujah!
The winds of hell have blown,
The world its hate hath shown,
Yet it is not overthrown,
Hallelujah for the cross!

Twas there the debt was paid,
Hallelujah! Hallelujah!
Our sins on Jesus laid,
Hallelujah! Hallelujah!
So round the cross we sing
Of Christ our offering,
Of Christ, our living King,
Hallelujah for the cross!

Hallelujah! Hallelujah!
Hallelujah for the cross!
Hallelujah! Hallelujah!
It shall never suffer loss!

Hallelujah for
The Cross
Horatius Bonar

XXXV

An Invitation

For what is a man profited, if he shall gain the whole world, and lose his own soul? Or what shall a man give in exchange for his own soul (Matthew 16:26)?

If we were to choose one word to describe the world's condition today, "restless" would be a good choice.

It seems that virtually everybody is frustrated with one thing or another. A lot of men don't like their jobs. Unfortunately, many are not totally satisfied with their spouses. Millions are frustrated because they believe their government does too much or not nearly enough.

In addition, many are seeking fulfillment in making money, gaining fame, pursuing political power, or acquiring a good education.

What would happen if some person in this world was totally satisfied with his/her job, was madly in love with his/her spouse, believed in all his government officials, was making plenty of money, felt he/she was getting more than adequate recognition for their accomplishments, was well-connected politically, and had more than enough education to accomplish whatever future goals they might want to pursue?

If we could find anybody who was honestly happy with all these situations, but he did not know Jesus Christ as Savior, what good would a few years of fleeting enjoyment be to him?

Be not afraid when one is made rich when the glory of his house is increased; For when he dieth *He shall carry nothing away:* his glory shall not descend after him (Psalm 49:16-17).

There are certain questions that we should all answer. At this point, let's consider two of them:

1. Are you inclined to believe things when you hear or read them from the Bible?
2. What good is it, if a man "gains the whole world," and *loses his own soul?*

These two questions are very important, especially as a person considers spiritual matters and eternal truths.

This chapter is an invitation to any reader who has not yet accepted Jesus Christ as his personal Savior. The invitation is to pay attention to the Gospel message, believe it, and be saved.

So what is the Gospel message? First, we must consider your present spiritual condition. Here's what the Scriptures say:

ALL have sinned.

For all have sinned, and come short of the glory of God (Romans 3:23).

As it is written, *There is none righteous, no not one* (Romans 3:10).

We all naturally want to defend ourselves, especially when it comes to something like accusations of sin! What does the Bible have to say about this?

The answer is unmistakably clear: we are all sinners. That includes your friends, this author, and you.

Are you willing to admit that you are a sinner?

Sin has extremely serious consequences.

For the wages of sin is death... (Romans 6:23a).

He that believeth not the Son *shall not see life; but the wrath of God abideth on him* (John 3:36b).

"Death," "shall not see life," and "wrath of God" all point to an eternity in hell for those who are not saved.

And whosoever was not found written in the book of life *was cast into the lake of fire* (Revelation 20:15.

Do you believe sin has these kinds of consequences?

A person cannot save himself.

For by grace are ye saved through faith. And that not of yourselves: it is the gift of God; *not of works, lest any man should boast* (Ephesians 2:8-9).

Do you believe the Bible is true when it says you cannot save yourself?

Notice figure 1 on the next page to see where you are spiritually.

Figure 1

Romans 3:23a All have sinned.

Romans 6:23; John 3:36; Revelation 20:15 Sin will send an unbeliever to hell.

Ephesians 2:8-9 A person cannot save himself.

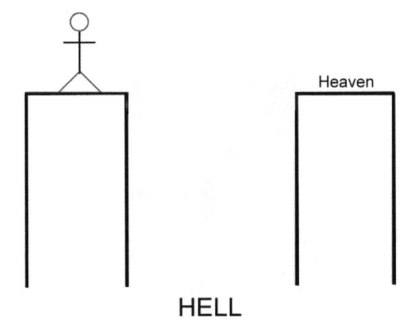

So far the message isn't very encouraging, is it?

We are all sinners; sin is going to send us to hell; and we can't save ourselves!

If this is all we knew about the Gospel, we would all be in an impossible position, but God has graciously provided the answer in His Son Jesus Christ!

Here is what the Bible has to say about God's solution:

1. Jesus paid the penalty for our sin.
    He is despised and rejected of men: a man of sorrow, and acquainted with grief: and we hid as it were our faces from Him; he was despised, and we esteemed Him not. Surely *He hath borne our griefs, and carried our sorrows;* yet we did esteem Him stricken, smitten of God, and afflicted. But *He was wounded for our transgressions,* He was bruised for our iniquities: the chastisement of our peace was upon Him; and with His stripes we are healed. All we like sheep have gone astray; we have turned every one to his own way; *and the Lord hath laid on Him the iniquity of us all* (Isaiah 53:3-6).

    But God commendeth His love toward us, in that, while we were yet sinners, *Christ died for us.* Much more then, being now justified by His blood, we shall be saved from wrath through Him (Romans 5:8-9).

    Either you will pay for your sin or Christ will.

    Do you believe He died for you?

2. Jesus is the ONLY One Who can save you.
    Jesus saith unto him, I am the way, the truth, and the life: *no man cometh unto the Father, but by Me* (John 14:6).

    Neither is there salvation in any other: for there is none other name under heaven given among men, whereby we must be saved (Acts 4:12).

    Religion says you must do something; Jesus, however, has already done it for you!

    Do you believe Jesus died for your sins?

If so, notice figure 2 on the next page to see where you are spiritually.

Figure 2

Isaiah 53:3-6; Romans 5:8-9 Jesus paid the penalty for our sin.

John 14:5; Acts 4:12 Jesus is the ONLY One Who can save you.

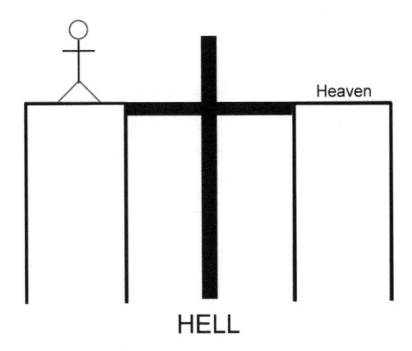

Next you must believe and repent:

1. Trust in God's grace to save you.
. Even when ye were dead in sins, hath quickened us together with Christ, *by grace ye are saved* (Ephesians 2:5).

Do you believe His grace is sufficient to save you?

2. Trust in the ability of Christ's blood to redeem you.
Forasmuch as ye know that ye were not redeemed with corruptible things, as silver and gold, from your vain conversation received by tradition from your fathers; But with *the precious blood of Christ, as of a Lamb without blemish and without spot* (I Peter 1:18-19).

Do you believe His blood can redeem you?

3. Trust in His resurrection to justify you.
But for us also, to whom it shall be imputed, if we believe on Him that raised up Jesus our Lord from the dead; Who was delivered for our offenses, and was *raised again for our justification* (Romans 4:24-25).

Do you believe His resurrection can justify you?

4. Repent of your sin.
Testifying both to the Jews, and also to the Greeks, *repentance toward God,* and faith toward our Lord Jesus Christ (Acts 20:21).

Actual saving faith and repentance are like two sides of a coin. When one repents he has the faith to believe he will be forgiven; and when one believes he realizes he is being saved from the awful condition of his sin!

Are you willing to repent of your sin?

Repentance means to totally change your mind and attitude toward sin. It involves your mind, emotions, and will. Are you willing to ask God to help you to avoid sin?

If you believe in God's grace, Christ's blood and resurrection, and are willing to repent, notice figure 3 on the next page to see where you are spiritually.

Figure 3

Ephesians 2:5 Trust in God's grace to save you.

I Peter 1:18-19 Trust in the ability of Christ's blood to redeem you.

Romans 4:24-25 Trust in His resurrection to justify you.

Acts 20:21 Repent of your sin.

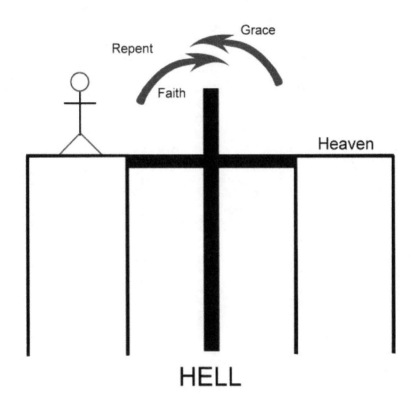

If you believe in these Biblical truths and are willing to repent, the only thing to do is accept Jesus as your personal Savior.

But as many as received Him, to them gave He power to become the sons of God even to them that believe on His name (John 1:12).

How do you do this?

The simplest way (already done by millions of believers) is to pray and ask Him to save you. Here is a sample prayer. If you sincerely pray these words or something that means the same thing, then you will immediately be saved!

Dear God, I come to you as a sinner. I know that I have sinned many times. I repent and ask you to forgive all my sin. I believe that Jesus died on the cross and rose again from the dead to save me. Jesus, save me now! Thank you for saving me. Thank you for all You've done. Help me to live for you the rest of my life. In Jesus' name, Amen.

Dear reader, please understand these words from Scripture:

The Lord is not slack concerning His promise, as some men count slackness; but is longsuffering to us-ward, *not willing that any should perish, but that all should come to repentance* (II Peter 3:9).

Are You Washed in The Blood?
Elisha A. Hoffman

Have you been to Jesus
For the cleansing power?
Are you washed in the blood of the Lamb?
Are you fully trusting in His grace this hour?
Are you washed in the blood of the Lamb?

Lay aside those garments
That are stained with sin,
And be washed in the blood of the Lamb!
There's a fountain flowing for the soul unclean,
O be washed in the blood of the Lamb!

If you prayed sincerely for Jesus to save you, please notice figure 4 to see where you are spiritually.

Figure 4

John 1:12 Receive Jesus as your personal Savior.

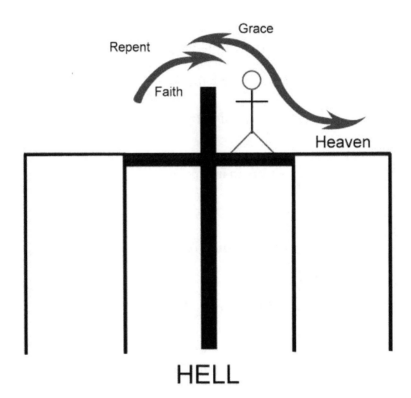

Questions or Comments?

Email the author at

eleutherosbooks@gmail.com

Ever wondered why the wording

of the New International Version

is different from the King James Version?

How about other translations?

Get answers in an upcoming book

entitled

Bible Translations: A Closer Look

Eleutheros Books

*If the Son therefore shall make you free, ye shall
be free indeed* **(John 8:36).**

Four quizzes, a test, and an answer key

The following pages contain a testing program suitable for Bible study groups, Christian day schools, Sunday School classes, or personal usage.

Quiz 1 is designed to cover the material in Section I.

Quiz 2 is designed to cover the material in Section II.

Quiz 3 is designed to cover the material in Section III.

Quiz 4 is designed to cover the material in Section IV.

The final exam covers the entire book.

An answer key is provided.

Quiz 1

True-False (write "T" or "F" to the left of each question)
1. The Bible is one of several sources to consult regarding our salvation.

2. We are "complete in Him" (Colossians 2:10).

3. God the Father has nothing to do with our salvation.

4. Believers are to do all to the glory of God (I Corinthians 10:31).

5. God is fair.

6. God can tolerate some sin.

7. All Christians agree on the details of the pre-science of our salvation.

8. Noah deserved deliverance from the flood.

9. Angels have the right to monitor God and His ways.

10. *Agape* love endures all things.

Multiple Choice (circle the correct response)
11. Which of the following is not true about the pre-science of our salvation?
A. God chose   B. God foreknew   C. God predestinated   D. all of these
E. none of these

12. Which of the following is true about God's foreknowledge?
A. it's the same as election   B. it's irrelevant to salvation
C. God knows some things   D. God foreknew who would be saved
E. none of these

13. Which of the following is not true about God's foreknowledge?
A. God foreknew the cross   B. God foreknew the possibility of certain events
C. God foreknew who would be saved   D. it applies only to Jewish converts
E. none of these

14. Which of the following is not true about election?
A. He chose to send His Son to the cross   B. He chose those who would be saved
C. He chose to create the world   D. He chose to give man a way to save himself
E. none of these

15. Which of the following is true about man?
    A. he is chosen by God   B. he is not responsible for his sin   C. he loved God first   D. he can rightly claim God made him to sin   E. none of these

16. God
    A. has a will   B. provides the way to be saved   C. inspired the Bible
    D. loves all people   E. all of these

17. The Greek verb "horkizo" means
    A. to tie a knot   B. to know all things   C. to mark off by boundaries
    D. to justify   E. none of these

Short Answer (place answers on the lines provided below)
18-20. List three reasons why God is not surprised when someone gets saved:

Reason 1 _____

Reason 2 _____

Reason 3 _____

Quiz 2

Matching (place response to the left of each question)

1. Sanctification
2. Sealing of the Holy Spirit
3. Spirit baptism
4. Indwelling of the Holy Spirit
5. Spiritual gifts
6. Propitiation
7. Filling of the Holy Spirit
8. Justification
9. Redemption
10. Regeneration

a. removal of wrath
b. an initiation
c. God gets all of the believer
d. "to make holy"
e. makes salvation's transaction official
f. the creation of new life
g. a purchase of blood
h. a declaration of righteousness
i. to give an offering
j. creates an ability to serve God
k. none of these

True-False (write "T" or "F" to the left of each question)

11. Our salvation requires a second work of grace.

12. The new birth is a necessity.

13. Sanctification is threefold: an accomplished fact, an ongoing process, and an ultimate reality.

14. Good works improves/completes justification.

15. We are free from the curse if we are saved.

Multiple Choice (circle the correct response)

16. Which of the following is <u>not</u> true about Spirit baptism?
    A. All believers are Spirit baptized   B. It's an accomplished fact for all believers
    C. It takes place after water baptism   D. It's not related to spiritual gifts
    E. None of these

17. Which of the following is true about adoption?
    A. Believers are dear children to God   B. It eliminates fear
    C. Believers have an "adult son" relationship with their heavenly Father
    D. All of these   E. None of these

18. Which of the following is true about a believer's priesthood?
    A. He must confess sins to a priest   B. He can pray to God only at certain times
    C. Christ is the believer's High Priest   D. It applies only to certain saints
    E. None of these

19. Which of the following is true about a believer's ambassadorship?
    A. It is for Christ   B. Ambassadors should speak boldly   C. The message is urgent
    D. The ambassador's testimony is important   E. All of these

20. Which of the following is not true about the filling of the Holy Spirit?
    A. It is a command for believers   B. It should be a continual state for believers
    C. It produces boldness in believers   D. It is directly related to spiritual gifts
    E. None of these

Quiz 3

True-False (write "T" or "F" to the left of each question)
1. The Greek word *houtos* means "in this way."

2. "Only begotten" refers to Jesus' special relationship to the Father and His ability to save the lost.

3. John 3:16 discusses both God's plan and provision for eternal life.

4. Jesus is the only one Who can save.

5. How much faith a person has is more important than where he places it.

6. David lived 5,000 years ago.

7. David prayed that God would restore his salvation.

8. All three Persons of the Trinity are involved in a believer's salvation.

9. Believers should not despise God's chastening (Job 5:17).

10. God's grace overpowers man's sin.

11. Believers can call God their Father.

12. Repentance is something done totally by man.

13. Jesus is the originator of our faith.

14. God will never abandon a believer.

15. Justification provides peace with God.

Multiple Choice (circle the correct response)
16. Which of the following is <u>not</u> true concerning a believer's inheritance?
    A. it is incorruptible   B. it is undefiled   C. it will fade away
    D. it is reserved in heaven   E. none of these

17. Which of the following is true about ultimate sanctification?
    A. it can happen in this life   B. it can be conferred by a church
    C. once enacted, it creates an eternally sinless condition
    D. it is for Old Testament saints only   E. none of these

18. Which of the following is true about glorification?
    A. it can't happen in this life   B. it is a total change in the bodies of believers
    C. it was planned by God before creation   D. all of these   E. none of these

19. Which of the following is not true about rewards?
    A. God will reward faithfulness   B. those who suffered for Jesus will be rewarded
    C. only church leaders will receive them
    D. both large and small deeds done for Jesus will be rewarded
    E. none of these

20. The word "eschatology"
    A. is a meaningless word   B. means "study (or doctrine) of the last things"
    C. means "study of creation"   D. means "study of salvation"
    E. none of these

\

Quiz 4

True-False (write "T" or "F" to the left of each question)
1. He Who hates sin died for the salvation of sinners.

2. Jesus is now only a mere human.

3. Satan is the spiritual father of unbelievers.

4. He Who is our high priest offered Himself as our sacrifice.

5. Christians have no reason to be humble.

6. The bodies of believers are likened to "the holy of holies" of the Old Testament temple.

7. God may become angry at sin which has already been forgiven.

8. Old Testament believers were saved by works.

9. Hammurabi's law code was written before the time of Moses.

10. The Law is useful in bringing people to Christ if it is properly applied.

Matching (place response to the left of each question)

11. ceremonial law	a. offerings
	b. to be observed after salvation
12. water baptism	c. the 10 commandments (Decalogue)
	d. property rights
13. civil law	e. to be done on the 8th day of life
	f. none of these
14. moral law	
15. circumcision	

Multiple Choice (circle the correct response)

16. Which of the following is true about God?
   A. He intended that the Law save   B. He works in our salvation eternally
   C. He allows believers to sin at will   D. He prays for bad things to happen
   E. none of these

17. Which of the following is <u>not</u> true about grace?
    A. God causes rain to fall on the just and unjust   B. it is crucial to justification
    C. it is multifaceted   D. God provides special grace as needed   E. none of these

18. Saving faith
    A. has an intellectual element   B. has an emotional element
    C. has a volitional element   D. must be in Christ   E. all of these

19. Old Testament believers
    A. needed God's grace   B. were saved by works
    C. were holier than New Testament believers   D. all of these   E. none of these

20. Which of the following is <u>not</u> true about repentance?
    A. it is essential to salvation   B. it is actually unrelated to faith
    C. it has an emotional element   D. it has its source in God's goodness
    E. none of these

Final Exam

True-False (write "T" or "F" to the left of each question)

1. Grace, faith, and the blood are important themes in both Old and New Testaments.

2. God provides salvation through several sources.

3. Anything that fails to glorify God is sin.

4. Jesus never talked about man's soul.

5. Jesus' blood has propitiated the Father's anger against sin.

6. The Holy Spirit indwells every believer.

7. Jesus left the grave in disarray after His resurrection.

8. Nobody ever touched Jesus after His resurrection.

9. Paul indicates that preaching is vain unless Jesus rose from the grave.

10. Jesus never foretold His resurrection.

11. The Gospels record that Jesus raised three other people from the dead (beside Himself).

12. Christ's blood has sanctifying power.

13. If Jesus had died of a heart attack, He could still save us.

14. Christ's blood was sinless.

15. God does not care that not all will repent.

16. Repentance involves a determination to forsake sin.

17. Both faith and repentance are crucial to salvation.

18. Repentance is primarily a sorrowful feeling.

19. Faith without works is dead.

20. Christians should defend their faith vigorously.

21. Joy is listed among the fruit of the Spirit.

22. Faith comes by hearing God's Word.

23. Faith ends when we reach heaven.

24. Faith manifests itself in various ways.

25. God's grace manifests itself in various ways.

26. God promises grace to arrogant people.

27. God promises grace to people in times of need.

28. God shows grace in sending rain on "the just and on the unjust."

29. Some people have been saved by keeping the Law.

30. There are various acceptable versions of the Gospel.

31. One of the main purposes of the Law was to expose man's sinfulness.

32. One of the main purposes of the Law was to bring people to Christ.

33. The New Testament has a relaxed view of morality when compared with the Old Testament.

34. Even though we are sinners, God has given believers responsible positions.

35. Jesus is both our High Priest and our sacrifice.

Multiple Choice (circle the correct response)

36. Which of the following will not be in heaven?
    A. a throne for Jesus   B. a throne for the Father   C. closed gates
    D. millions of redeemed souls   E. none of these

37. Which of the following is true?
    A. heaven will eventually decay   B. Jesus could rapture the Church today
    C. the new Jerusalem is about the size of Chicago   D. hell is not a real place
    E. none of these

38. Which of the following is true about Israel?
    A. All Jews will reign with Christ   B. Israel will suffer forever
    C. the Apostles will rule over its 12 tribes   D. all of these   E. none of these

39. God gives rewards based on
    A. what our parents did   B. whatever things we do selfishly   C. His anger
    D. His justice and love   E. none of these

40. God will give a crown of righteousness to those who
    A. love His appearing   B. ignore His Word   C. pray when it's convenient
    D. worship angels   E. none of these

Matching (place response to the left of each question)

41. Sealing	A. God declares a believer to be righteous
42. Indwelling of Holy Spirit	B. often gives believer boldness to serve God
43. Sanctification	C. implantation of a new life principle
44. Redemption	D. initiation into the body of Christ
45. Justification	E. involves teaching, conviction of sin, other things
46. Filling of the Spirit	F. God's stamp of approval on salvation
47. Glorification	G. a purchase accomplished by Christ's blood
48. Spirit baptism	H. removal of God's wrath
49. Propitiation	I. joy of angels in heaven
50. Regeneration	J. "to make holy"
	K. none of these

Discussion

51-60. Discuss any doctrine of salvation and its importance in your spiritual life.

The Ramifications of Our Salvation
Answer Key

Quiz 1   1. False 2. True 3. False 4. True 5. False 6. False 7. False 8. False
         9. False 10. True 11. E 12. D 13. D 14. D 15. A 16. E 17. C
         18-20. Election, foreknowledge, predestination (in any order)

Quiz 2   1. D 2. E 3. B 4. K 5. J 6. A 7. C 8. H 9. G 10. F 11. False
         12. True 13. True 14. False 15. True 16. C 17. D 18. C 19. E
         20. D

Quiz 3   1. True 2. True 3. True 4. True 5. False 6. False 7. False 8. True
         9. True 10. True 11. True 12. False 13. True 14. True 15. True
         16. C 17. C 18. D 19. C 20. B

Quiz 4   1. True 2. False 3. True 4. True 5. False 6. True 7. False 8. False
         9. True 10. True 11. A 12. B 13. D 14. C 15. E 16. B 17. E
         18. E 19. A 20. B

Final   1. True 2. False 3. True 4. False 5. True 6. True 7. False 8. False
Exam   9. True 10. False 11. True 12. True 13. False 14. True 15. False
         16. True 17. True 18. False 19. True 20. True 21. True 22. True
         23. False 24. True 25. True 26. False 27. True 28. True 29. False
         30. False 31. True 32. True 33. False 34. True 35. True 36. C
         37. B 38. C 39. D 40. A 41. F 42. E 43. J 44. G 45. A 46. B
         47. K 48. D 49. H 50. C 51-60. Give full credit if the student can explain
         any soteriological doctrine correctly and can explain its significance in his/her
         life.

Suggested   Count one point for each question on the four quizzes. Four quizzes x 20
Grading   points = 80 points. Count two points for each question on the final exam.
Scale   60 questions x 2=120 points. 80 + 120= 200 points for the course.

            A reasonable grading scale would be the following: A (90-100%, 0-20
            missed points)   B (80-89%, 21-40 missed points)   C (70-79%, 41-60
            missed points)   D (60-69%, 61-80 missed points)   F (anything lower
            than a "D")

CPSIA information can be obtained
at www.ICGtesting.com
Printed in the USA
BVHW03s0246070718
521024BV00001B/3/P